Herbal Magic

2023
WEEKLY PLANNER
JULY 2022 – DECEMBER 2023

ROCK POINT

2023 Year at a Glance

JANUARY

S	M	T	W	T	F	S
	1	2	3	4	5	6	7
1	2	3	4	5	6	7
8	9	10	11	12	13	14
15	16	17	18	19	20	21
22	23	24	25	26	27	28
29	30	31				

FEBRUARY

S	M	T	W	T	F	S
			1	2	3	4
5	6	7	8	9	10	11
12	13	14	15	16	17	18
19	20	21	22	23	24	25
26	27	28				

MARCH

S	M	T	W	T	F	S
			1	2	3	4
5	6	7	8	9	10	11
12	13	14	15	16	17	18
19	20	21	22	23	24	25
26	27	28	29	30	31	

APRIL

S	M	T	W	T	F	S
						1
2	3	4	5	6	7	8
9	10	11	12	13	14	15
16	17	18	19	20	21	22
23	24	25	26	27	28	29
30						

MAY

S	M	T	W	T	F	S
	1	2	3	4	5	6
7	8	9	10	11	12	13
14	15	16	17	18	19	20
21	22	23	24	25	26	27
28	29	30	31			

JUNE

S	M	T	W	T	F	S
				1	2	3
4	5	6	7	8	9	10
11	12	13	14	15	16	17
18	19	20	21	22	23	24
25	26	27	28	29	30	

JULY

S	M	T	W	T	F	S
						1
2	3	4	5	6	7	8
9	10	11	12	13	14	15
16	17	18	19	20	21	22
23	24	25	26	27	28	29
30	31					

AUGUST

S	M	T	W	T	F	S
		1	2	3	4	5
6	7	8	9	10	11	12
13	14	15	16	17	18	19
20	21	22	23	24	25	26
27	28	29	30	31		

SEPTEMBER

S	M	T	W	T	F	S
					1	2
3	4	5	6	7	8	9
10	11	12	13	14	15	16
17	18	19	20	21	22	23
24	25	26	27	28	29	30

OCTOBER

S	M	T	W	T	F	S
1	2	3	4	5	6	7
8	9	10	11	12	13	14
15	16	17	18	19	20	21
22	23	24	25	26	27	28
29	30	31				

NOVEMBER

S	M	T	W	T	F	S
			1	2	3	4
5	6	7	8	9	10	11
12	13	14	15	16	17	18
19	20	21	22	23	24	25
26	27	28	29	30		

DECEMBER

S	M	T	W	T	F	S
					1	2
3	4	5	6	7	8	9
10	11	12	13	14	15	16
17	18	19	20	21	22	23
24	25	26	27	28	29	30
31						

2024 Year at a Glance

JANUARY

S	M	T	W	T	F	S
	1	2	3	4	5	6
7	8	9	10	11	12	13
14	15	16	17	18	19	20
21	22	23	24	25	26	27
28	29	30	31			

FEBRUARY

S	M	T	W	T	F	S
				1	2	3
4	5	6	7	8	9	10
11	12	13	14	15	16	17
18	19	20	21	22	23	24
25	26	27	28	29		

MARCH

S	M	T	W	T	F	S
					1	2
3	4	5	6	7	8	9
10	11	12	13	14	15	16
17	18	19	20	21	22	23
24	25	26	27	28	29	30
31						

APRIL

S	M	T	W	T	F	S
	1	2	3	4	5	6
7	8	9	10	11	12	13
14	15	16	17	18	19	20
21	22	23	24	25	26	27
28	29	30				

MAY

S	M	T	W	T	F	S
			1	2	3	4
5	6	7	8	9	10	11
12	13	14	15	16	17	18
19	20	21	22	23	24	25
26	27	28	29	30	31	

JUNE

S	M	T	W	T	F	S
						1
2	3	4	5	6	7	8
9	10	11	12	13	14	15
16	17	18	19	20	21	22
23	24	25	26	27	28	29
30						

JULY

S	M	T	W	T	F	S
	1	2	3	4	5	6
7	8	9	10	11	12	13
14	15	16	17	18	19	20
21	22	23	24	25	26	27
28	29	30	31			

AUGUST

S	M	T	W	T	F	S
				1	2	3
4	5	6	7	8	9	10
11	12	13	14	15	16	17
18	19	20	21	22	23	24
25	26	27	28	29	30	31

SEPTEMBER

S	M	T	W	T	F	S
1	2	3	4	5	6	7
8	9	10	11	12	13	14
15	16	17	18	19	20	21
22	23	24	25	26	27	28
29	30					

OCTOBER

S	M	T	W	T	F	S
		1	2	3	4	5
6	7	8	9	10	11	12
13	14	15	16	17	18	19
20	21	22	23	24	25	26
27	28	29	30	31		

NOVEMBER

S	M	T	W	T	F	S
					1	2
3	4	5	6	7	8	9
10	11	12	13	14	15	16
17	18	19	20	21	22	23
24	25	26	27	28	29	30

DECEMBER

S	M	T	W	T	F	S
1	2	3	4	5	6	7
8	9	10	11	12	13	14
15	16	17	18	19	20	21
22	23	24	25	26	27	28
29	30	31				

BASIL (LEAVES)

floral, licorice flavor; love, money spells, protection

HIBISCUS (BLOSSOMS)

fruity, floral flavor; attracting love, Moon magic, intuition

CHAMOMILE (BLOSSOMS)

apple-honey flavor; comfort, patience, sleep

LAVENDER (BLOSSOMS)

sweet, floral, herbal flavor; cleansing, devotion, peace, calm, intelligence, happiness

ECHINACEA (BLOSSOMS)

strong, tongue-tingling, straw-like flavor; inner strength, immunity

LEMON BALM (LEAVES)

herbal lemony flavor; sympathy

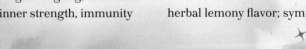

LEMON THYME AND COMMON THYME (LEAVES)

herbal lemon flavor; woodsy, pungent flavor; beauty, courage, good health, prevent nightmares, protection, remove negative energy, sleep

PASSIONFLOWER (LEAVES)

mild, grassy, floral flavor; relaxation, soothes strong emotions, hospitality

LEMON VERBENA (LEAVES AND BLOSSOMS)

lemon-lime flavor; inspiration

ROSE (HIPS, SPENT BLOOMS)

sweet floral flavor; immunity boost, love

MINT (LEAVES)

cooling, slightly peppery flavor; clear and meaningful communication, refreshment, travel

ROSEMARY (LEAVES)

strong pine-like flavor; clarity, remembrance, sweet dreams, purification

JULY 2022

NOTES	SUNDAY	MONDAY	TUESDAY
	3	4	5
		INDEPENDENCE DAY (US)	
	10	11	12
	17	18	19
	24	25	26
	31		

JULY 2022

WEDNESDAY	THURSDAY	FRIDAY	SATURDAY
		1 CANADA DAY (CAN)	2
6	◖ 7	8	9
● 13	14	15	16
◗ 20	21	22	23
27	○ 28	29	30

MOONWORT | *Lunaria annua*

PLANETARY COMPANION	**DAILY CORRESPONDENCE**
MOON	MONDAY
ZODIAC SIGN	**ELEMENT**
Cancer	WATER
ENERGY	
FEMININE	

Also called honesty, money plant, or silver dollar plant, as its silver dollar–shaped pods are said to turn into actual silver when tucked away in a closet, this moonwort is a different plant than *Botrychium lunaria*, the endangered fern. This magic herb, brought to the colonies by the Pilgrims, speaks of forgetfulness, which can also be interpreted as forgiveness, and speaks honestly and sincerely. This plant easily seeds itself, offering a compound return on your initial investment. It's a great plant with which to introduce kids to gardening because it is fast growing and bears money-shaped seed pods.

MAGICAL PROPERTIES
Moonwort promises prosperity and encourages honesty, and its silver-dollar pods evoke the Moon. When needed, it can also repel the odd monster or two.

SUGGESTED USE
Use moonwort in all Moon magic spells, prosperity spells, and when the need for honest communication is required. Dried stalks make interesting additions to wreaths and flower arrangements. Tuck the dried pods into money charms, or sprinkle the Moon-shaped seeds under a child's bed to ward off lurking monsters who interrupt sweet dreams. Tuck some seeds into your pocket for luck at the casino or neighborhood poker game.

Moon-shaped seeds and Moonbeam wishes
fend off monsters faster than kisses!
Call on moonwort's silver charms to keep me safe from monsters' harm.
Jingle, jangle go the seeds, scaring monsters off indeed.

JUNE / JULY 2022

MONDAY (JUNE) 27

TUESDAY (JUNE) 28

WEDNESDAY (JUNE) 29

THURSDAY (JUNE) 30

FRIDAY CANADA DAY (CAN) 1

SATURDAY 2

SUNDAY 3

JULY 2022

MONDAY INDEPENDENCE DAY (US)   4

TUESDAY   5

WEDNESDAY   6

THURSDAY   7

FRIDAY 8

SATURDAY 9

SUNDAY 10

With bay in hand I proudly stand before
the goddess realm to thank you for the
path you've strewn with guidance, grit,
and more for glory to the sisterhood
of those who came before.

JULY 2022

MONDAY 11

TUESDAY 12

⬤ WEDNESDAY 13

THURSDAY 14

FRIDAY 15

SATURDAY 16

SUNDAY 17

When spirits sag and energies wane a friend's embrace can oft sustain. Sweet William's face is filled with joy, a song of cheer, a needed refrain.

JULY 2022

MONDAY 18

TUESDAY 19

WEDNESDAY 20

THURSDAY 21

FRIDAY 22

SATURDAY 23

SUNDAY 24

*Where basil leaves its scented trail,
life's meant to be devoured. I call upon
sweet basil's charm to heed my honest
plea to garnish life with extra spice and
increased spending power.*

JULY 2022

MONDAY   25

TUESDAY   26

WEDNESDAY   27

○ THURSDAY   28

FRIDAY   **29**

SATURDAY   **30**

SUNDAY   **31**

When melancholy strikes, blue borage
I do seek to bathe my spirit with its spell,
to heal my weary soul.
For borage blooms can lift the cloud,
return me to my peak.

WISHES AND DREAMS JAR

Whether wishing for that new person in your life or dreaming of your future with the one you have, a wishes and dreams jar can capture the magic and preserve it to multiply. Alter the herbs, flowers, and crystals based on the energy or wish that you seek to attract to you.

Select a Mason jar with a lid, as large or as small as you like. Then, if your wish is to be married, for example, gather:

- Basil for luck and love

- Bee balm for compassion

- Dill for good cheer

- Ivy for marriage

- Lavender for undying devotion

- Oregano for joy

- Rosemary for remembrance

- Sage for wisdom

- Yarrow for courage and everlasting love

Add:

- ꙮ Garnet for passion
- ꙮ Rose petals for romance
- ꙮ Your wishes written on a bay leaf

If the timing is right, place your items in a basket and infuse them overnight with the power of the New Moon to set your intentions.

Place the items in the jar, seal the jar, and place it on your altar, or other place you can see it, to be reminded of your wishes and dreams. When passing by, take a moment to reflect on your desires and say quietly or aloud:

Sweet herbs, do work for me, that life as married I may be,

with all emotions so bestowed when life doth take the bumpy road

I know my heart will still be true and

love grows then beyond what's new.

When you have time, or to refresh your spell, light a red candle, gaze into the flame, and imagine your married life as you dream it. Extinguish the candle safely. Take a breath and thank the herbs and crystals for their work.

AUGUST 2022

NOTES	SUNDAY	MONDAY	TUESDAY
		1	2
		SUMMER BANK HOLIDAY (UK-SCT)	
	7	8	9
	14	15	16
	21	22	23
	28	29	30
		SUMMER BANK HOLIDAY (UK-ENG/NIR/WAL)	

AUGUST 2022

WEDNESDAY	THURSDAY	FRIDAY	SATURDAY
3	4	5	6
10	11	12	13
17	18	19	20
24	25	26	27
31			

APPLE BLOSSOM | *Malus domestica*

PLANETARY COMPANION	DAILY CORRESPONDENCE
VENUS	**FRIDAY**
ZODIAC SIGN	ELEMENT
Taurus	**WATER**
ENERGY	
FEMININE	

Even before the sweet, juicy fruit appears, the apple tree offers its healing blossoms for your herbal magic. An edible bloom, in the language of flowers, apple blossom indicates preference. Variously a symbol of immortality, of the dead, and of health and vitality, the apple and its blossom have a lot to offer. An apple tree in full bloom is Nature smiling—when the blooms scatter on the wind, listen for her laughter.

MAGICAL PROPERTIES
Apple blossoms are joyous tools to call for love, garden magic/harvest, beauty, health, and fertility.

SUGGESTED USE
Plant an apple tree in your herb garden to guarantee a fruitful harvest—both herbs and apples—and provide a sanctuary to sit and contemplate the wonder that is Nature. Brew an apple blossom infusion, let it cool, and wash your face with it to instantly increase your beauty and attract that one true love. Press and dry the blossoms and tuck them into a love note. Scatter the blossoms over your altar to honor Venus. Cast a circle of apple blossoms around a pink candle and light the candle to attract your lover.

A healthy herbal harvest is all but guaranteed as I scatter
apple blossoms as far as I can see.
They fertilize with happiness and guard against the weeds,
so herbs grow lush and full and strong—thank you, apple tree.

AUGUST 2022

MONDAY SUMMER BANK HOLIDAY (UK-SCT) 1

TUESDAY 2

WEDNESDAY 3

THURSDAY 4

FRIDAY 5

SATURDAY 6

SUNDAY 7

AUGUST 2022

MONDAY 8

TUESDAY 9

WEDNESDAY 10

THURSDAY 11

FRIDAY 12

SATURDAY 13

SUNDAY 14

I place this birch broom by my door
to sweep away the dust and more,
where lightning strikes or evil looms,
my broom so swift protects these rooms.

AUGUST 2022

MONDAY 15

TUESDAY 16

WEDNESDAY 17

THURSDAY 18

FRIDAY

19

SATURDAY

20

SUNDAY

21

Sprig of mint, dash of cloves, basil leaf,
and nutmeg whole, season well my résumé
that fruitful interviews come my way.
Let offers bloom like hawthorn trees that
I may choose the job I please.

AUGUST 2022

MONDAY 22

TUESDAY 23

WEDNESDAY 24

THURSDAY 25

FRIDAY 26

○ **SATURDAY** 27

SUNDAY 28

With bundle of chives I sweep the air free
of anything lurking to harm.
With sprinkle of chives the message is clear:
Evil is not welcome here.
With blossom of chives I garnish my home
and so have set this charm.

POPPETS

Magical poppets are an ancient tradition that are intended to focus our intentions and carry our magical wishes to the Universe. The poppet represents, or is connected to, the person for whom the magic spell is intended. Magical belief says that any magic acted upon the poppet will be felt by the person it represents. You can cut old cloth into shapes (perhaps trace a gingerbread cookie cutter to start, if that suits you), sew up the edges, and stuff it with dried herbs and flowers. Make yarn dolls and weave in dried herbal sprigs and blossoms, or come up with your own creative representation in which you can incorporate herbs and their powers. Use sticks, leaves, and other natural materials to make "stick figure" poppets, for example. Poppets can be used plain and as is, or decorated as elaborately as you like with crystals, flowers, or herbs to further your intentions; add scent with essential oils to boost your spell's energy, based on intentions, desired spell outcomes, or correspondence to a specific person.

1. Gather all the materials you need, including dried herbs and flowers for stuffing.

2. Cleanse the materials with a sprinkle of salt and a moment of thanks for their previous work, as well as a moment of gratitude for the work to be done.

3. Assemble the poppet as desired, imbuing each material you use with the desired outcomes and intention of the spell.

4. Hold the finished poppet in your hands and infuse it with your spirit and warmth. Visualize the spell and desired outcome your poppet will work toward on your behalf. Say quietly or aloud:

Of image made to speak of truth that heart and mind unite

of healing [loving, lucky, truthful, protective, etc.] herbs and other charms for energies ignite

that which you dream and hope brings near to grab hold

of with delight.

5. Place the poppet on your altar, if you wish, or other appropriate space while you wait for the spell to manifest.

6. When finished with your poppet, as you cleansed it with salt to start, sprinkle it with a bit more salt to cleanse it from its current associations. Take a moment to acknowledge its work.

7. Dispose of it appropriately. If the poppet is made of all-natural materials, dismantle and dispose of it accordingly: recycle, bury, burn safely, reuse, etc. If not, dispose of it in the trash.

SEPTEMBER 2022

NOTES	SUNDAY	MONDAY	TUESDAY
	4	5	6
	FATHER'S DAY (AUS/NZ)	LABOR DAY (US) LABOUR DAY (CAN)	
	11	12	13
	PATRIOT DAY (US) GRANDPARENTS' DAY (US)		
	18	19	20
	○ 25	26	27
	ROSH HASHANAH (BEGINS AT SUNDOWN)		

SEPTEMBER 2022

WEDNESDAY	THURSDAY	FRIDAY	SATURDAY
	1	2	3
7	8	9	10
14	15	16	17
	FIRST DAY OF NATIONAL HISPANIC HERITAGE MONTH		
21	22	23	24
	FALL EQUINOX		
28	29	30	

CINQUEFOIL | *Potentilla simplex*

PLANETARY COMPANIONS	DAILY CORRESPONDENCE
MERCURY, VENUS	**WEDNESDAY, FRIDAY**
ZODIAC SIGN	ELEMENT
Gemini	**FIRE**
ENERGY	
MASCULINE	

In the language of flowers, cinquefoil speaks of maternal love. It is an old herb with a long history of medicinal and magical uses. The plant's characteristic five leaves are said to represent wisdom, health, power, love, and money, making it an all-purpose herbal charm. Also known as five-finger grass, cinquefoil is usually the ingredient in potions calling for "fingers."

MAGICAL PROPERTIES
Cinquefoil calls prophetic dreams to you, can be used to call love to your life, and is said to lure fish to your net for a hearty catch.

SUGGESTED USE
Carry cinquefoil in a charm bag to activate its five energies: money, love, power, health, and wisdom. Place in a dream pillow for prophetic dreams and expanded intuition. Use in protection spells.

Early to bed and early to rise is said to make one
healthy, wealthy, and wise.
But what about power and much-needed love?
Add cinquefoil to the mix and reap all the above.

AUGUST/SEPTEMBER 2022

MONDAY (AUGUST) SUMMER BANK HOLIDAY (UK-ENG/NIR/WAL) **29**

TUESDAY (AUGUST) **30**

WEDNESDAY (AUGUST) **31**

THURSDAY **1**

FRIDAY **2**

SATURDAY **3**

SUNDAY FATHER'S DAY (AUS/NZ) **4**

SEPTEMBER 2022

MONDAY LABOR DAY (US) / LABOUR DAY (CAN)   5

TUESDAY   6

WEDNESDAY   7

THURSDAY   8

FRIDAY 9

SATURDAY 10

SUNDAY PATRIOT DAY (US) / GRANDPARENTS' DAY (US) 11

With caraway I bless this house
that it becomes a home
where love and faith and trust
abound and fear does
never roam.

SEPTEMBER 2022

MONDAY 12

TUESDAY 13

WEDNESDAY 14

THURSDAY NATIONAL HISPANIC HERITAGE MONTH BEGINS 15

FRIDAY   16

SATURDAY   17

SUNDAY   18

So drunk in love I wish to be, I sip this catnip
and rose tea whilst sitting near camellia tree
adorned with blossoms pleading thee, do nip my
earlobe playfully and tell me, undeniably,
how unable you are to resist me.

SEPTEMBER 2022

MONDAY 19

TUESDAY 20

WEDNESDAY 21

THURSDAY FALL EQUINOX 22

FRIDAY 23

SATURDAY 24

○ **SUNDAY** ROSH HASHANAH (BEGINS AT SUNDOWN) 25

These garlic cloves I chew for luck are sure to cast their spell. To curry favor from the gods as well as from their smell, which casts an aura far and wide encouraging luck to swell.

MAGIC AND FAIRIES IN THE HERB GARDEN

Fairies can be mystical, magical, and charming, or impish, troublesome, and a real bother. An herb garden is a magical place, with its visual beauty and tantalizing aromas and tastes, but attracting sweet-tempered fairies into your garden can be tricky. Creating a homey atmosphere is the best place to start.

Fairies are minimalists when it comes to living needs—shelter and water are their most basic ones. The base of a tree, or a simple toadstool, can suffice for shelter, and the morning dew sleeping on your plants' leaves refreshes like nectar from the gods, especially lady's mantle. The hawthorn is said to be among their favorite trees, with its white flowers signaling a return of the fairies in late spring. Oak and ash trees are able substitutes. No trees? Think herbs and flowers that grow tall and sturdy. Leaves of the zucchini plant in your garden are a natural shelter, as is rosemary or sage.

To make certain the invitation to take up residence in your garden is well received, keep these tips in mind as you try to tempt the fairies in.

BE KIND. Fairies favor those who care for and nurture the Earth and keep its creatures happy . . . feed the birds; be kind to all wildlife. Keep up with your garden chores, like weeding and cleaning up plant decay, to keep things tidy and healthy.

BE INVITING. Invite fairies into your garden with kind thoughts and deeds. When you're out working among the plants, invite the fairies to work alongside you in harmony with Nature, or point out specific plants they may like . . . a lush carpet of elfin thyme for napping, bright marigolds to serve as lanterns, or beautiful bee balm as a source of refreshing tea.

BE PROTECTIVE. Provide shelter . . . a fairy is at home in Nature, so include plants in your herb garden with large leaves or other features to provide shelter from the Sun and rain.

BE NURTURING. As for all of Nature, water is a must . . . a birdbath or butterfly pond will enchant and delight as a spot for bathing and drinking.

BE FUN. Fairies love bling. If you can, place some crystals in your garden or a reflective gazing ball. Music helps, too. Wind chimes can tempt with their soothing charms. Bell-shaped flowers invite the fairies to play their own tunes.

BE GRATEFUL. Offerings of fresh-cut herbs, especially milk and honey, are believed to be especially welcoming. These extra touches, as you would do for any guest in your home, are sure to delight.

OCTOBER 2022

NOTES	SUNDAY	MONDAY	TUESDAY
	2 ◗	3	4
			YOM KIPPUR (BEGINS AT SUNDOWN)
	9 ●	10	11
	SUKKOT (BEGINS AT SUNDOWN)	INDIGENOUS PEOPLES' DAY (US) / COLUMBUS DAY (US) / THANKSGIVING DAY (CAN)	
	16	17 ◑	18
		SIMCHAT TORAH (BEGINS AT SUNDOWN)	
	23	24	25 ○
		LABOUR DAY (NZ)	
	30	31	
		HALLOWEEN	

OCTOBER 2022

WEDNESDAY	THURSDAY	FRIDAY	SATURDAY
			1
5	6	7 LABOUR DAY (AUS-ACT/NSW/SA)	8
12	13	14	15
19	20	21	22
26	27	28	29

HIBISCUS | *Hibiscus sabdariffa*

PLANETARY COMPANION	DAILY CORRESPONDENCE
VENUS	**FRIDAY**
ZODIAC SIGN	ELEMENT
Scorpio	**WATER**
ENERGY	
FEMININE	

A part of the mallow family, hibiscus speaks of delicate beauty. It is associated with Moon magic and feminine energies.

MAGICAL PROPERTIES

Hibiscus is usually the go-to herb for spells of lust, love, beauty, and marriage; it can also be used for divination and dream magic and as a balm to soothe tired spirits.

SUGGESTED USE

Float hibiscus flowers, lavender blossoms, and rose buds in a ritual bath for a healthy dose of self-love. Or place the same combination of blossoms in a large bowl filled with water when scrying, especially when divining love and the identity of your true love. Hibiscus makes a lovely, fruity tea that can offer a respite of calm in a harried day, allowing you to refresh and recharge. A facial steam with hibiscus flowers will enhance your natural beauty.

These flowers bold unfurl, unfold, their beauty to behold.
Their leaves for tea reveal to me love's future as it's told.

SEPTEMBER / OCTOBER 2022

MONDAY (SEPTEMBER) — 26

TUESDAY (SEPTEMBER) — 27

WEDNESDAY (SEPTEMBER) — 28

THURSDAY (SEPTEMBER) — 29

FRIDAY (SEPTEMBER) — 30

SATURDAY — 1

SUNDAY — 2

OCTOBER 2022

MONDAY 3

TUESDAY YOM KIPPUR (BEGINS AT SUNDOWN) 4

WEDNESDAY 5

THURSDAY 6

FRIDAY LABOUR DAY (AUS-ACT/NSW/SA) 7

SATURDAY 8

● **SUNDAY** SUKKOT (BEGINS AT SUNDOWN) 9

To tackle dust and dirt and grime your mighty
scent does shine. To cleanse, protect, and heal
my home, I turn at once to pine.

OCTOBER 2022

MONDAY INDIGENOUS PEOPLES' DAY (US)/COLUMBUS DAY (US) / THANKSGIVING DAY (CAN) 10

TUESDAY 11

WEDNESDAY 12

THURSDAY 13

FRIDAY 14

SATURDAY 15

SUNDAY 16

Prepare the ground have I to receive this
bleeding heart, to cradle, raise, and nurture well
its blooming true love song. For when I spy its
sweet love charms and hear their winsome tune
my heart responds with joyful verse and hope
for new love soon.

OCTOBER 2022

 MONDAY SIMCHAT TORAH (BEGINS AT SUNDOWN) **17**

TUESDAY **18**

WEDNESDAY **19**

THURSDAY **20**

FRIDAY   21

SATURDAY   22

SUNDAY   23

*A dash of pepper starts the spell; a sprinkle keeps
me safe from evil eyes and other harms that do
invade my space. With sprinkle, dash, and even
more, keep all unwanted from my door.*

OCTOBER 2022

MONDAY LABOUR DAY (NZ)   24

○ **TUESDAY**   25

WEDNESDAY   26

THURSDAY   27

FRIDAY   28

SATURDAY   29

SUNDAY   30

I ask the Sun and Moon to bless these seeds I wish to grow.
To warm and coax, encourage, and feed to spread their
roots below, while reaching limbs to Sun-filled skies and
welcoming the rain. Abundant harvest, lush and strong,
each herb sings its refrain.

SEASON YOUR LIFE WITH FRIENDSHIP

Gather your friends on a Sun-filled day to celebrate the bounty of your garden—or just to celebrate the bounty of your friendship. Have plenty of herbs, fresh, dried, or still potted or plotted—on hand that support love and friendship, encourage growth and open communication, and that are just joyous to experience and behold. Kitchen gifts of food and wine made with fresh herbs you have grown will enhance the celebratory spirit of the circle. Consider including these herbs in your herbal friendship ritual, whose energies attract and maintain friendship, or speak the language of friendship:

- Apples
- Cloves
- Lavender
- Lemon balm
- Lemons
- Myrtle
- Oak-leaved geranium
- Rose
- Rosemary
- Sweet pea
- Zinnia, for absent friends

Cast a ritual circle by strewing herbs and blossoms around your gathering area, inside or out. Casting is simply connecting with the energies of the Earth and Universe. Invite your friends to step inside the circle to connect and amplify their energies by joining hands. If you like, each person can place an herbal offering inside the circle. The purpose of your circle is to celebrate and honor the goddess, Mother Earth, and all her gifts and to open yourself to her energies, increasing vibration and intuition. Invite her to join you in the circle.

Use the circle for intention setting. Create and chant your own mantra to raise the energies around you. Stand or sit silently in meditation on your intentions. Sing, walk, or dance clockwise in the circle. Why clockwise? The spinning clockwise energy brings things to you. Share intentions aloud, or offer them quietly to the Universe.

When it is time to close the circle, light a candle in memory of someone unable to be there and take a moment to give thanks for the seasonal blessings of the Earth and your friends. Walk or dance counterclockwise, which dispels or banishes the energy, to dissolve the circle.

Blessed be.

This circle of friends is the circle of life.

May these herbal gifts present both soothe and delight

that the goddess we call does indeed shine her light

to bless all here in friendship that forever burns bright.

NOVEMBER 2022

NOTES	SUNDAY	MONDAY	TUESDAY
			1
			ALL SAINTS' DAY
	6	7	8
	DAYLIGHT SAVING TIME ENDS (US/CAN)		ELECTION DAY (US)
	13	14	15
	20	21	22
	27	28	29

NOVEMBER 2022

WEDNESDAY	THURSDAY	FRIDAY	SATURDAY
2	3	4	5
9	10	11 VETERANS DAY (US)	12
16	17	18	19
23	24 THANKSGIVING DAY (US)	25 NATIVE AMERICAN HERITAGE DAY (US)	26
30			

PEPPERMINT | *Mentha × piperita*

PLANETARY COMPANIONS **VENUS, MERCURY**	**DAILY CORRESPONDENCE** **FRIDAY, WEDNESDAY**
ZODIAC SIGNS Virgo, Aquarius	**ELEMENT** **AIR**
ENERGY **FEMININE**	

Named after Minthe, the Greek nymph beloved by Hades, who was turned into an infertile mint plant (which thrives by creeping and crawling its way through your garden) by his jealous wife, Persephone, peppermint tells of warm feelings. This popular herb finds many applications in various industries and is especially beloved for culinary uses—its leaves have been a cherished source of tea through the centuries.

MAGICAL PROPERTIES
A cleansing herb, mint clears the mind, boosts concentration, and increases intuitive focus. It can relieve headaches, ease troubling thoughts, and promote renewal.

SUGGESTED USE
Mint's fresh scent will keep pests from your cupboards. Brew a cup of mint tea and take a moment to clear your mind when tough decisions loom. Grow near your doorway for its protective properties, or hang bundles in doorways and near windows to cleanse negative energies from the home. Anoint a white candle with peppermint essential oil and burn before a cleansing ritual. Fill a dream pillow with peppermint, place it over your eyes, and use it to clear negative thoughts, expand intuition, increase focus on your intentions, and induce prophetic dreams. Place near crystals or other magic tools used to cleanse and recharge their energies.

I strew this mint across my floor to cleanse the air of germs and more,
to clear the mind where cobwebs brew and stimulate fresh thoughts anew.

MONDAY (OCTOBER) HALLOWEEN   31

TUESDAY ALL SAINTS' DAY   1

WEDNESDAY   2

THURSDAY   3

FRIDAY   4

SATURDAY   5

SUNDAY DAYLIGHT SAVING TIME ENDS (US/CAN)   6

NOVEMBER 2022

MONDAY 7

TUESDAY ELECTION DAY (US) 8

WEDNESDAY 9

THURSDAY 10

FRIDAY VETERANS DAY (US) 11

SATURDAY 12

SUNDAY 13

With a sprinkle, a dash, a pinch or
two of secret spice of tannish hue
I hereby cast out evil harm and
do invoke protective charm.

NOVEMBER 2022

MONDAY   14

TUESDAY   15

WEDNESDAY   16

THURSDAY   17

FRIDAY   18

SATURDAY   19

SUNDAY   20

With sweetly spicy leaves of cilantro near,
I savor each as I repeat the spell for health so dear:
Give me your gently healing charm that I may
grow each day, inhale good form to weather storms,
emerging like a ray of Sun whose warming beams
do soothe and dry away the tears.

NOVEMBER 2022

MONDAY 21

TUESDAY 22

○ **WEDNESDAY** 23

THURSDAY THANKSGIVING DAY (US) 24

FRIDAY NATIVE AMERICAN HERITAGE DAY (US)

25

SATURDAY

26

SUNDAY

27

Where fairies tread and spirits roam, pine needle
mats provide a home. For animals who guard
and guide, keep watch with their protective eye.
Sweet juniper and cedar, too, whose whispers
calm, defend, and soothe.

SELF-LOVE AFFIRMATION

Romantic love is grand, but the truest kind of love is self-love. It's the love that sees our flaws, features, gifts, dreams, and failures without judgment, with full acceptance, and says, "I see you for all that makes you *you*. I celebrate you. I honor you. I value you. I love you."

Self-love can be tough to come by . . . we tend to be hard on ourselves. This is your opportunity to practice self-love affirmations, opening your heart to all other loves in your life. Think of what a wonderful life it will be.

Rose quartz, the love crystal, will energize any herb you select that has energies of love and healing for this affirmation, such as dill, rosemary, lavender, rose, chamomile, red clover, marjoram, and many more. Place the herb sprigs in a vase by your bed.

As you ready for sleep, hold the rose quartz in your hands. Feel its warmth. Take a few deep inhales of the chosen herbs, feeling the scent fill you from head to toe with love and acceptance as you inhale, and releasing any self-doubt or criticism as you exhale. When ready, say quietly or aloud three times before falling asleep:

I open my heart to love. I am love. I am loved. I am loving.

I love myself for all that I am and all that I do.

FERTILE CAULDRON

The cauldron, traditional symbol of the hearth, also represents the womb, fertility, transformation, and rebirth. If your wish is to become pregnant, there is no better tool to incorporate into your magic.

Along with your cauldron, gather a green candle, matches, water (for fire safety), and herbs to promote lust (for fun) and fertility (for your wish), such as acorns, apple blossom, cilantro, dill, geranium, ginseng, ivy, lady's mantle, and parsley.

Time your spell to the New Moon or Full Moon, cast it on a Monday, and invite your favorite goddess (Venus is a good choice) to join.

Set the cauldron on a heatproof surface and place the candle and herbs next to it. Light the candle. Take a moment to visualize your new little one and how it will feel to hold your baby. When ready, one at a time, drop the herbs into the cauldron and say quietly or aloud, repeating as needed, until all the herbs are used:

The fertile Earth has given birth to each and every herb.

With powers ripe to stir new life—each bloom, each leaf, and seed—

within the Earth to bloom again as much as within me.

O' Moon and goddess, do unite to grant my wish indeed.

DECEMBER 2022

NOTES	SUNDAY	MONDAY	TUESDAY
	4	5	6
	11	12	13
	18	19	20
	HANUKKAH (BEGINS AT SUNDOWN)		
	25	26	27
	CHRISTMAS DAY	BOXING DAY (UK/CAN/AUS/NZ) KWANZAA	

DECEMBER 2022

WEDNESDAY	THURSDAY	FRIDAY	SATURDAY
	1 WORLD AIDS DAY	2	3 INTERNATIONAL DAY OF PERSONS WITH DISABILITIES
● 7	8	9	10 HUMAN RIGHTS DAY
14	15	◗ 16	17
21 WINTER SOLSTICE	22	○ 23	24 CHRISTMAS EVE
28	◖ 29	30	31 NEW YEAR'S EVE

BERGAMOT, WILD | *Monarda fistulosa*

PLANETARY COMPANION	**DAILY CORRESPONDENCE**
MARS	TUESDAY
ZODIAC SIGNS	**ELEMENT**
Gemini, Virgo	AIR
ENERGY	
FEMININE	

Bergamot's sweet message is one of irresistibility. Its aromatic leaves found widespread use as a substitute for tea in New England after Boston's infamous Tea Party. Bergamot's showy flowers are a natural garden lure for bees, butterflies, and hummingbirds, making it a favorite of the garden fairies, too.

MAGICAL PROPERTIES
Bergamot beckons love, purification, protection, intuition, and restorative sleep.

SUGGESTED USE
Use dried leaves for herbal infusions that may be helpful in meditation. Its lovely scent makes it a prime candidate for use in potpourris, dream sachets, or tussie-mussies. Inhale the fragrance and exhale its sweet scent imbued with your intentions. Burn a red candle while drinking the tea for love spells. Gather the flowers into a bath sachet and surrender your tensions to the soothing water and calming energies of this herb.

With each warm sip I seek to see beyond the worldly realm.
To understand the joy at hand when those we seek to shun
give us their hand, their hearts, their stand to join us all as one.

NOVEMBER/DECEMBER 2022

MONDAY (NOVEMBER) 28

TUESDAY (NOVEMBER) 29

WEDNESDAY (NOVEMBER) 30

THURSDAY WORLD AIDS DAY 1

FRIDAY 2

SATURDAY INTERNATIONAL DAY OF PERSONS WITH DISABILITIES 3

SUNDAY 4

DECEMBER 2022

MONDAY   5

TUESDAY   6

WEDNESDAY   7

THURSDAY   8

FRIDAY

9

SATURDAY HUMAN RIGHTS DAY

10

SUNDAY

11

I bless these cloves with friendship deep and
true and call on love's great power that the
message reaches you. For ties that bind in love
and life cannot be yet undone. As time goes by
it pulls our hearts still closer, as if one.

DECEMBER 2022

MONDAY 12

TUESDAY 13

WEDNESDAY 14

THURSDAY 15

FRIDAY   16

SATURDAY   17

SUNDAY   HANUKKAH (BEGINS AT SUNDOWN)   18

Sunny flower, "tooth of lion," infuse in me
the strength of iron.
Fill my heart with courage so free and
steep in me the will to see.

DECEMBER 2022

MONDAY 19

TUESDAY 20

WEDNESDAY WINTER SOLSTICE 21

THURSDAY 22

○ **FRIDAY** 23

SATURDAY CHRISTMAS EVE 24

SUNDAY CHRISTMAS DAY 25

*Sweet herbs and blooms whose charms
doth soothe, engage me in debate,
for anger's rising fast inside and tempting
me to hate. Do fill me with your calming
voice to take up anger's place.*

PREPARING CANDLES TO WORK THEIR MAGIC

*A*s you do with crystals, cleansing or blessing your candles and infusing them with your intentions sets the stage for the burning candle to release that energy into the Universe. Stay present in the moment, noticing any thoughts, feelings, or sensations.

Set your intention: Clearly and confidently, holding your candle in both hands, focus on the feeling as you visualize your intention, through the candle's burning energy, coming to fruition.

LEAD WITH GRATITUDE: Take a moment to thank the candle and the Universe for the work they are about to undertake on your behalf.

ANOINT WITH OIL: Choose an essential oil that complements your intentions and add a drop or two to the outside of the candle, if desired.

GARNISH WITH HERBS: Use the herbs you've selected for this specific intention. Rub the oil-coated candle in the herbs, create an herb circle around the candle (keep fire safety in mind), or place them in a vase nearby or on your altar. Tied with a color-matching ribbon, herbs make a lovely offering to any goddess you may invite to join you.

Take a deep breath. You're ready to ask the Universe to grant your wishes, powered by a spell or spoken plainly, yet truthfully, from the heart.

WHEN YOU DON'T GET THE . . .

Job, promotion, raise, marriage proposal, date, win, vote . . . you name it, whatever you yearn for but don't manifest can stop your momentum fast. Maybe it wasn't meant to be, or maybe the timing's just wrong—whatever the Universe's reason, now is not the time to give up and withdraw. Take stock of what's important and create a spell jar to reflect your intentions and dreams.

With leaf of courage and seed for luck,

sprig of truth and bark for trust,

I fill this jar with wishes true that next time when my time is due,

the Universe delights with me in granting wishes dear to me.

JANUARY 2023

NOTES	SUNDAY	MONDAY	TUESDAY
	1	2	3
	NEW YEAR'S DAY	BANK HOLIDAY (UK-SCT)	
	8	9	10
	15	16	17
		CIVIL RIGHTS DAY MARTIN LUTHER KING JR. DAY (US)	
	22	23	24
	CHINESE NEW YEAR		
	29	30	31

JANUARY 2023

WEDNESDAY	THURSDAY	FRIDAY	SATURDAY
4	5 ●	6	7
11	12	13 ◗	14
18	19	20 ○	21
25	26 AUSTRALIA DAY	27 ◖ HOLOCAUST REMEMBRANCE DAY	28

FOXGLOVE | *Digitalis purpurea*

PLANETARY COMPANIONS	DAILY CORRESPONDENCE
VENUS, SATURN	**FRIDAY, SATURDAY**
ZODIAC SIGN	ELEMENT
Taurus	**WATER**
ENERGY	
FEMININE	

Due to its toxicity, this dangerous plant is purely ornamental, and a delightful specimen it is. Another garden favorite of bees, butterflies, hummingbirds—and fairies—foxglove is a traditional cottage garden and witch's garden plant. Its original name, folksglove, arose from the fact that the flowers resemble the fingers of a glove and referred to the "good folk," the fairies who dwell deep within the forest where "folksglove" grew. Its bell-shaped flowers can be heard tolling if you have fairies living amongst your herbs.

MAGICAL PROPERTIES
Foxglove is an herb of protection.

SUGGESTED USE
Plant foxglove in your garden to summon fairy protection.

Where unseen evil bides its time to unleash all its woe,
it's foxglove's warning bells that ring their silent call to arms.
Swift fairies swarm to guard your home and
keep you safe from harm.

DECEMBER/JANUARY 2023

MONDAY (DECEMBER) BOXING DAY (UK/CAN/AUS/NZ)/ KWANZAA — 26

TUESDAY (DECEMBER) — 27

WEDNESDAY (DECEMBER) — 28

THURSDAY (DECEMBER) — 29

FRIDAY (DECEMBER) — 30

SATURDAY (DECEMBER) NEW YEAR'S EVE — 31

SUNDAY NEW YEAR'S DAY — 1

JANUARY 2023

MONDAY BANK HOLIDAY (UK-SCT)   2

TUESDAY   3

WEDNESDAY   4

THURSDAY   5

FRIDAY 6

SATURDAY 7

SUNDAY 8

*It's luck of the Irish I need at this time
and clover is sure to deliver.
Though three-leaved, not four, you've done
it before, with your charms great good
fortune comes hither.*

JANUARY 2023

MONDAY

9

TUESDAY

10

WEDNESDAY

11

THURSDAY

12

FRIDAY   13

SATURDAY   14

SUNDAY   15

A journey calls and I must go, but comfrey
comes along to keep the luck of travel
smooth and sailing winds blow strong.
With comfrey in my pocket, safe return
cannot go wrong.

JANUARY 2023

MONDAY CIVIL RIGHTS DAY/ MARTIN LUTHER KING JR. DAY (US) 16

TUESDAY 17

WEDNESDAY 18

THURSDAY 19

FRIDAY 20

○ **SATURDAY** 21

SUNDAY CHINESE NEW YEAR 22

O' fairest fern, I call on you
to spread your fairy wings
to keep me safe from evil spells
and other harmful things.

JANUARY 2023

MONDAY   23

TUESDAY   24

WEDNESDAY   25

THURSDAY AUSTRALIA DAY   26

FRIDAY HOLOCAUST REMEMBRANCE DAY   27

SATURDAY   28

SUNDAY   29

Allspice, all good, all wishes
are buried with you.
Unleash your rich fragrance
into the world that my world
becomes richer for it.

STRESS SOOTHER

A little stress can be an inspiring motivator, but when the pressure builds and threatens to derail you, take a breather to regain your balance. Several herbal allies can help—the most fragrant engage as many senses as possible to reground. Choose from these or others you prefer: black tea, chamomile, ginger (to sip); borage, lavender (to bathe); rosemary, oregano (to burn or season); willow, verbena (to cast a circle or meditate with). Close your eyes, if you feel comfortable, inhale the herbs' rejuvenating scents, and breathe out the stress of the moment. Repeat as needed. When ready, say quietly or aloud:

Your calming scents do ease my stress and soothe my cares away.

Your leaves relieve my thoughts that tease and tempt my sanity.

Your stems stand strong, to urge me on, to stand and face the fray.

WHEN EMOTIONS BLOCK CREATIVITY

Sometimes the creative energy just gets stuck . . . stuck behind a dam of negative energy blocking its free flow. When that happens, whether for work or play, the reason might not be obvious. Take a minute to assess your mood. If you feel your energy, or self-esteem, needs a positive boost, try this:

Sit beneath a willow, if you can, or gather a branch. You can also use nasturtium, or any gold-yellow-orange-colored blossoms you have available. Make a circle around a yellow candle with the willow branch or herbs and safely light the candle. Gaze into the flame and feel the warmth of the sunny colors surrounding you heighten your energy—imagine it flowing from your mind to your hands, ears, mouth, feet, and toes. Let it swirl inside until it bursts forth with joy. When ready, say quietly or aloud:

The light within shines bright, with creativity.

Like flame to wax, it melts and shifts, revealing what's inside.

With willow wand I call it forth to use again with pride.

FEBRUARY 2023

NOTES	SUNDAY	MONDAY	TUESDAY
	● 5	6	7
	WAITANGI DAY (NZ)	WAITANGI DAY OBSERVED (NZ)	
	12	◐ 13	14
			VALENTINE'S DAY
	19	○ 20	21
		PRESIDENTS' DAY (US)	
	26	◑ 27	28

FEBRUARY 2023

WEDNESDAY	THURSDAY	FRIDAY	SATURDAY
1 FIRST DAY OF BLACK HISTORY MONTH	2 GROUNDHOG DAY (US/CAN)	3	4
8	9	10	11
15	16	17	18
22 ASH WEDNESDAY	23	24	25

JASMINE | *Jasminum officinale*

PLANETARY COMPANION
MOON

DAILY CORRESPONDENCE
MONDAY

ZODIAC SIGNS
Cancer, Capricorn,
Pisces, Sagittarius

ELEMENT
WATER

ENERGY
FEMININE

The intoxicating scent of jasmine tells of friendliness and sweet love. It is the herb of attraction. Its influence is powerful. Jasmine's scent, it's said, opens the eyes and heart to the beauty in all things—and to see beyond the superficial beauty that is fleeting.

MAGICAL PROPERTIES
Call on jasmine for love spells and divination.

SUGGESTED USE
Incorporate jasmine into any Moon magic spells or rituals, especially during the waxing phase. Include the blossoms in love charms. Savor the scent of jasmine before bed to encourage prophetic dreams.

With blossoms sweet before my eyes,
the future told, may I behold, with jasmine at my side.

JANUARY/FEBRUARY 2023

MONDAY (JANUARY)   30

TUESDAY (JANUARY)   31

WEDNESDAY FIRST DAY OF BLACK HISTORY MONTH   1

THURSDAY GROUNDHOG DAY (US/CAN)   2

FRIDAY   3

SATURDAY   4

SUNDAY WAITANGI DAY (NZ)   5

FEBRUARY 2023

MONDAY WAITANGI DAY OBSERVED (NZ)   6

TUESDAY   7

WEDNESDAY   8

THURSDAY   9

FRIDAY 10

SATURDAY 11

SUNDAY 12

From wise men once an honored gift,
so valued are your ways. Burn frankincense
to cleanse the air and usher out the haze that
spirit guides may whisper wise and healing
words this day.

FEBRUARY 2023

MONDAY 13

TUESDAY VALENTINE'S DAY 14

WEDNESDAY 15

THURSDAY 16

FRIDAY **17**

SATURDAY **18**

SUNDAY **19**

With ivy crown and silken gown and veil
of pure intent, my pledge today will never
stray beyond our covenant.

FEBRUARY 2023

○ **MONDAY** PRESIDENTS' DAY (US)　　　　　　　　　**20**

TUESDAY　　　　　　　　　**21**

WEDNESDAY ASH WEDNESDAY　　　　　　　　　**22**

THURSDAY　　　　　　　　　**23**

FRIDAY 24

SATURDAY 25

SUNDAY 26

*O' sunny marigold, do shine your luck
on me this day, that judgment due at
any time is rendered such my way.*

SWEET DREAMS

Whether for a much-needed restful night's sleep to repair and recharge, diving into a deep state of intuitive sleep to call forth prophetic dreams, or tapping into your intuition for problem solving, your herb garden is full of support.

Among the many herbal helpers available, try angelica, borage, jasmine, lavender, marigold, moonflower, moonwort, mugwort, mullein, peppermint, rose petals, sandalwood, vervain, and yarrow to find which herb, or combination of herbs, works for you. Tucked into a dream sachet, sprinkled into a bath, placed under your pillow or beside your bed, or sipped as a calming tea, as appropriate, the key to unlocking sleepy slumber or messages from the angels is yours to discover.

Sweet sleep, I call you to my side to revel in your charms.

Sweet sleep, I need your seeing eye to warn of coming harm.

Sweet sleep, with guiding eloquence, awaken my sixth sense.

LAVENDER WAND FOR SOOTHING SPELLS

If your lavender crop is in full bloom, or your farmers' market is tempting you, put your harvest to good use with a lavender wand. A wave of the softly scented lavender wand can cast magic in many directions. The meditative rhythm of weaving the ribbon is as soothing as the scents emanating from the wand.

GATHER:
Odd number of fresh, long-stemmed lavender blooms
    (at least 12 inches, or 30 cm; make sure the blooms are dry)
6-foot (1.8-m) length of ¼-inch (6-mm) ribbon

1. Strip the leaves from the stems (save for potpourri or other uses). Bundle the stems together, aligning the bottom of the flower blooms. Wrap the ribbon around the stems right under the blooms and tightly tie a knot.

2. Turn the bundle upside down (blooms pointing down) and gently bend the lavender stems down, at the ribbon's edge, over the blossoms, covering them.

3. Begin weaving the ribbon under and over the stems all around the stalk and covering the blooms. When you reach the last stem in your weave, continue to weave more rows of ribbon under, over, and around, working down the stems and gently pushing the ribbon up tight against the previous row, covering the blooms fully.

4. When you reach the end of the blooms, wrap the ribbon around the stems as far as you like to finish and tie a bow where you stop.

5. Let your wand dry for a few days, then adjust the weaving and wrapping as needed to tighten a bit.

Tuck the wand under your pillow to call soothing sleep to you, or hang in a closet, place in a drawer, or decorate a wall with your wand until needed. When the time is right (say, in tune with the Moon's last quarter) and a bit of calm is needed in your frenzied world, put your lavender wand to use.

MARCH 2023

NOTES	SUNDAY	MONDAY	TUESDAY
	5	6	● 7
		PURIM (BEGINS AT SUNDOWN)	
	12	13	14
	DAYLIGHT SAVING TIME BEGINS (US/CAN)	LABOUR DAY (AUS-VIC)	
	19	20 ○	21
	MOTHERING SUNDAY (UK)	SPRING EQUINOX	NOWRUZ
	26	27 ◖	28

MARCH 2023

WEDNESDAY	THURSDAY	FRIDAY	SATURDAY
1 FIRST DAY OF WOMEN'S HISTORY MONTH	2	3	4
8	9	10	11
15	16	17 ST. PATRICK'S DAY	18
22 RAMADAN (BEGINS AT SUNDOWN)	23	24	25
29	30	31	

MOONFLOWER | *Ipomoea alba*

PLANETARY COMPANION	DAILY CORRESPONDENCE
MOON	**MONDAY**
ZODIAC SIGN	ELEMENT
Cancer	**WATER**
ENERGY	
FEMININE	

A type of Datura, moonflower has a nocturnal nature that reveals dreams of love in its meaning. It is the ultimate representation of the beautiful emerging from darkness—and thriving. The enchanting white flowers open in late afternoon, as darkness hovers and the Moon begins to show, and stay open for one night only . . . the opposite of the day lily or the morning glory, to which the moonflower is related. The flowers' scent, which attracts their moth pollinators, is not one all humans can detect. Consider your herbal energies in full display if you can. **Note:** This plant is poisonous and is best incorporated into an herbal Moon garden for inviting pollinators and encouraging the magical growth cycle.

MAGICAL PROPERTIES
As a flower ruled by the Moon, moonflower is a must for any herbal Moon garden, to use in Moon spells, and for divination, dreams, and intuition.

SUGGESTED USE
Under the light of the Full Moon, inhale moonflower's perfume to induce prophetic dreams and awaken your intuition. As a Moon flower, incorporate it into your Esbat ritual, as you wish.

For herbs at this hour have magic and
power beyond when the Sun's in the sky.
In darkness you see, reveal unto me,
your prophecy, truth, and desire.

FEBRUARY/MARCH 2023

MONDAY (FEBRUARY) 27

TUESDAY (FEBRUARY) 28

WEDNESDAY FIRST DAY OF WOMEN'S HISTORY MONTH 1

THURSDAY 2

FRIDAY 3

SATURDAY 4

SUNDAY 5

MARCH 2023

MONDAY PURIM (BEGINS AT SUNDOWN)   6

TUESDAY   7

WEDNESDAY   8

THURSDAY   9

FRIDAY   10

SATURDAY   11

SUNDAY DAYLIGHT SAVING TIME BEGINS (US/CAN)   12

Sweet marjoram, whose tiny leaves belie their
magic might, do waft and weave your scented
charms to keep my home from plight.

MARCH 2023

MONDAY LABOUR DAY (AUS-VIC)   13

TUESDAY   14

WEDNESDAY   15

THURSDAY   16

FRIDAY ST. PATRICK'S DAY

17

SATURDAY

18

SUNDAY MOTHERING SUNDAY (UK)

19

Moon-shaped seeds and Moonbeam wishes fend off
monsters faster than kisses! Call on moonwort's silver
charms to keep me safe from monsters' harm. Jingle,
jangle go the seeds, scaring monsters off indeed.

MONDAY SPRING EQUINOX | **20**

TUESDAY NOWRUZ | **21**

WEDNESDAY RAMADAN (BEGINS AT SUNDOWN) | **22**

THURSDAY | **23**

FRIDAY   24

SATURDAY   25

SUNDAY   26

*When parsley peeks its perky head upon my
windowsill, I'm quick to use it any way to keep us
safe from ills. Eat up, my friends, and thank this
herb for its magic ways. For luck, and health,
and fertile wealth, parsley does fulfill.*

THIEVES' THERAPEUTIC TONIC

The legendary thieves' vinegar, also known as Marseilles vinegar, could be a welcome tonic in today's turbulent time. This ultimate in DIY kitchen magic was reputedly developed by a band of enterprising thieves during Europe's seventeenth-century Black Plague. Their protective herbal concoction, as told to us by René-Maurice Gattefossé—widely regarded as the father of aromatherapy—in his 1937 book, *Aromathérapie,* combined the natural cleansing attributes of vinegar with the magical herbal properties of *wormwood, meadowsweet, wild marjoram, sage, fifty cloves, two ounces of campanula roots, two ounces of angelica, rosemary, horehound, and three large measures of camphor.*

And, yes, a regular dousing in the vinegar potion did, indeed, keep these particular bandits healthy against the plague . . . seems it also repels fleas—a suspected carrier of the plague . . . but did not prevent their arrest, upon which they credited their health to the vinegar and bartered the recipe in exchange for their freedom (or so legend says).

With a typical base of apple cider vinegar, today's recipes vary widely in herbs used, but its purpose remains the same: one of protection—from evil to the common cold. Modern herbal combinations often call for black pepper, cinnamon, clove, garlic, juniper berry, lavender, rosemary, sage, and thyme, or a combination. Make your own therapeutic tonic to address whatever plagues you.

GATHER:

1 head garlic, cloves halved or roughly chopped

2 tablespoons each (weight varies) 4 fresh or dried herbs (one herb for each thief!)
     from the original recipe (skip the camphor) or the modern version, plus
     additional herbs as desired for flavor or intention

4 cups (960 ml) apple cider vinegar (preferably organic)

1. In a clean quart-size (960-ml) Mason jar, combine the garlic and herbs. Pour in the vinegar to come almost to the top of the jar. Use the clean handle of a wooden spoon to stir the mixture, coaxing out any air bubbles.

2. Place a piece of parchment paper over the mouth of the jar and seal the lid. Let its magical properties multiply anywhere you normally store your vinegars for about a month, shaking daily to distribute the herbs.

3. Strain the vinegar into a clean jar, pressing on the herbs to extract as much vinegar as possible, and seal the jar. Compost the herbs, if you can, and thank the Earth for their healing properties.

Ideas for use include in any recipe calling for vinegar, as part of a salad dressing, mix to taste into sparkling water for a refreshing tonic, splash some behind your ears in a nod to the thieves, or use as part of a natural cleaning solution—but be sure to test surfaces first to ensure the acid in the vinegar does not damage them. Before using, say quietly or aloud:

Protective potion, heed my plea, whose spicy scented help I seek.

Do cloak me in your healing charms—

protect me from life's many harms.

APRIL 2023

NOTES	SUNDAY	MONDAY	TUESDAY
	2	3	4
	PALM SUNDAY		
	9	10	11
	EASTER		
	16	17	18
	ORTHODOX EASTER	YOM HASHOAH (BEGINS AT SUNDOWN)	
	23	24	25
	30		ANZAC DAY (AUS/NZ)

APRIL 2023

WEDNESDAY	THURSDAY	FRIDAY	SATURDAY
			1 APRIL FOOLS' DAY
5 PASSOVER (BEGINS AT SUNDOWN)	● **6**	**7** GOOD FRIDAY	**8**
12 ◗	**13**	**14**	**15**
19 ○	**20**	**21** EID AL-FITR (BEGINS AT SUNDOWN)	**22** EARTH DAY
26 ◖	**27**	**28**	**29**
ADMINISTRATIVE PROFESSIONALS' DAY (US)			

ORANGE BLOSSOM | *Citrus sinensis*

PLANETARY COMPANION **SUN**	DAILY CORRESPONDENCE **SUNDAY**
ZODIAC SIGN Leo	ELEMENT **FIRE**
ENERGY **FEMININE**	

The orange flower represents chastity and speaks quite clearly when included in a wedding bouquet—it reflects your loveliness. Like the deliciously refreshing fruit the flower becomes, orange blossom uplifts, soothes, and rejuvenates.

MAGICAL PROPERTIES
Orange blossom brings happiness to our lives. It attracts friendship, love, luck, joy, and abundance and stirs up a sunny outlook on life.

SUGGESTED USE
Carry orange blossom in a wedding bouquet to ensure wedded bliss. Add to potpourri to be given as gifts of friendship to cement the bond. Use orange flower water as part of your facial cleansing routine for a fresh start to each day. Dress an orange candle with orange essential oil before burning to ease the blues and let the sunshine in. Wear orange blossom to attract luck and love to you.

A whiff of orange from blossom true does
signal sweet my love for you.
These petals tossed upon us rain like tears of joy,
a sweet refrain,
our marriage sealed, it's ever true,
this rare unending love of two.

MONDAY (MARCH) 27

TUESDAY (MARCH) 28

WEDNESDAY (MARCH) 29

THURSDAY (MARCH) 30

FRIDAY (MARCH) 31

SATURDAY APRIL FOOLS' DAY 1

SUNDAY PALM SUNDAY 2

APRIL 2023

MONDAY 3

TUESDAY 4

WEDNESDAY PASSOVER (BEGINS AT SUNDOWN) 5

● THURSDAY 6

FRIDAY GOOD FRIDAY   7

SATURDAY   8

SUNDAY EASTER   9

*Beautiful rose, as your petals unfurl, attract my
heart's desire. Delicate rose, as your beauty does
grow, may your charms unleashed inspire a
passion so bright it lights up the night and
extinguishes never nor tires.*

APRIL 2023

MONDAY   10

TUESDAY   11

WEDNESDAY   12

◗ THURSDAY   13

FRIDAY 14

SATURDAY 15

SUNDAY ORTHODOX EASTER 16

Candle white, burn so bright, reveal your
healing message now. Aloe gel, join this
spell, reach deep within your curing well
of healing balm and soothing calm that
everything will soon be well.

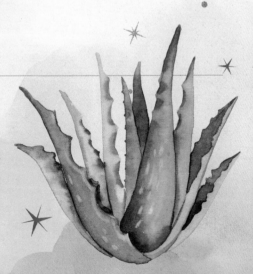

APRIL 2023

MONDAY YOM HASHOAH (BEGINS AT SUNDOWN)   17

TUESDAY   18

WEDNESDAY   19

○ **THURSDAY**   20

FRIDAY EID AL-FITR (BEGINS AT SUNDOWN)

21

SATURDAY EARTH DAY

22

SUNDAY

23

With sandalwood and candles three,
I light your flames with prayer to free
my wishes into space, where they'll swift
manifest and come to me.

APRIL 2023

MONDAY   24

TUESDAY ANZAC DAY (AUS/NZ)   25

WEDNESDAY ADMINISTRATIVE PROFESSIONALS' DAY (US)   26

THURSDAY   27

FRIDAY   28

SATURDAY   29

SUNDAY   30

An angel's kiss has blessed this herb,
as Nature's story tells, an angel's grace is
sought this day, protective, true, and bold.
To usher evil out the door, I cast this
charming spell.

ROSE PETAL HEALING RITUAL

Although the first thing you may associate with roses is love, they have enormous power to heal as well, especially when mind and spirit are heavy with burden.

For this ritual, gather as many rose petals as you can . . . from your garden, if you're lucky enough to have them growing, from a grocer or farmers' market, leftover from a gift . . . along with a large bowl full of water, a green candle, a heatproof container for the candle, and matches.

1. In a quiet area where you won't be disturbed, outdoors if you can—near a body of water, small or large (omit the bowl of water then)—cast a circle with the rose petals near the water, saving 5 to 10 petals. If you are not near water, place the bowl of water in the center of the circle along with the candle and reserved rose petals.

2. Step into the circle with gratitude for the opportunity to learn from your pain. Take a moment to set your intention to release your burdens and be open to healing. When ready, light the candle and sit next to the water.

3. One at a time, pick up a rose petal. Hold it in your hand and appreciate its soft, soothing feel and scent. Visualize it absorbing the burden you wish to let go. When you are ready to let go of the burden, float the petal in the water, watching it drift away from you. Repeat the exercise with the remaining petals, infusing each with a different burden, or the same, if it is extremely weighty.

4. When all the petals are in the water, carrying your burdens away, say quietly or aloud:

On water calm these petals soft do float

my pain away.

With one deep breath I release the rest

that healing starts this day.

FINDING A NEW HOME

When wishing, dreaming, pining for a place to call home, a little herbal magic for luck can't be a bad idea. Fire up your cauldron and "cook" a nice herbal stew as a housewarming present to yourself.

In your cauldron, combine as many of the following as you can. As you add each ingredient to season your wish for a new home, picture what that home looks like and how you will feel living in it.

FOR WISHES GRANTED: basil, bay laurel, black tea, catnip, cinnamon, clover, dandelion, ginseng, jasmine, lavender, marjoram, pine, sage, sunflower, violet

FOR HOME: aloe, angelica, chamomile, chrysanthemum

FOR HEARTH GODDESS WISDOM: call on Brigid, Freya, Hecate, Hestia

FOR NEW BEGINNINGS: birch

FOR A LITTLE LUCK: nutmeg

FOR PROTECTION: mistletoe

Place the herb-filled cauldron under the Full Moon's magic light and offer the following, quietly or aloud:

These herbs all from the Earth I've plucked,

to sprinkle dreams with fertile luck.

For home and hearth and nest I seek

to grow my limbs and plant my feet,

To settle into life sublime, please show me

hearth and home that's mine.

MAY 2023

NOTES	SUNDAY	MONDAY	TUESDAY
		1 LABOUR DAY (AUS-QLD) EARLY MAY BANK HOLIDAY (UK) FIRST DAY OF ASIAN AMERICAN AND PACIFIC ISLANDER HERITAGE MONTH	2
	7	8	9
	14 MOTHER'S DAY (US/CAN)	15	16
	21	22 VICTORIA DAY (CAN)	23
	28	29 SPRING BANK HOLIDAY (UK) MEMORIAL DAY (US)	30

MAY 2023

WEDNESDAY	THURSDAY	FRIDAY	SATURDAY
3	4 ●	5	6
		CINCO DE MAYO	
10	11 ◐	12	13
17	18 ○	19	20
24	25	26 ◖	27
31			

SAGE, COMMON | *Salvia officinalis*

PLANETARY COMPANIONS
MOON, JUPITER

DAILY CORRESPONDENCE
MONDAY, THURSDAY

ZODIAC SIGNS
Sagittarius, Taurus

ELEMENT
AIR

ENERGY
MASCULINE

An herb with a long history of healing use, sage will bring you wise counsel—its very name speaks of wisdom and healing. Sage also speaks of all things domestic and the virtues thereof. White sage, historically and traditionally used ceremonially by Native American peoples in smudging ceremonies, is in danger due to overcollection; common sage is a suitable stand-in for this purpose and as its best if you've grown it yourself. When sage blossoms in your garden, it beckons hummingbirds to join.

MAGICAL PROPERTIES
Sage is used to ease grief from the loss of a loved one; promote health and longevity; and grant wisdom, protection, and wishes.

SUGGESTED USE
Include sage in sympathy arrangements for comfort and healing. Mix dried sprigs and leaves into potpourris for its cleansing energies. Burn a black candle dressed with sage essential oil for cleansing negative energies from your home. Create an infusion of sage water. Sprinkle it with a sage sprig anywhere protection from evil energy is needed.

With sheath of sage I do entreat the wisdom I do need
to sift the seeds of want and need for that which I desire,
and heed the universal truth that less is more indeed.

MAY 2023

MONDAY	LABOUR DAY (AUS-QLD) / EARLY MAY BANK HOLIDAY (UK) / FIRST DAY OF ASIAN AMERICAN AND PACIFIC ISLANDER HERITAGE MONTH	1
TUESDAY		2
WEDNESDAY		3
THURSDAY		4
FRIDAY	CINCO DE MAYO	5
SATURDAY		6
SUNDAY		7

MAY 2023

MONDAY 8

TUESDAY 9

WEDNESDAY 10

THURSDAY 11

FRIDAY 12

SATURDAY 13

SUNDAY MOTHER'S DAY (US/CAN) 14

This flower tucked into my bed reveals my fate to me. When dreamt upon, this magic charm will show who marries me.

MAY 2023

MONDAY 15

TUESDAY 16

WEDNESDAY 17

THURSDAY 18

○ **FRIDAY**   19

SATURDAY   20

SUNDAY   21

With patience I do steep and brew the heart
of my intent in you that empty cup may signal
true great riches that are overdue.

MAY 2023

MONDAY VICTORIA DAY (CAN)   **22**

TUESDAY   **23**

WEDNESDAY   **24**

THURSDAY   **25**

FRIDAY   ✳   **26** ✳

SATURDAY   ✳   **27**

SUNDAY   **28**

*Sweet viola, whose face does enchant, turn
your lovely gaze my way that no harm
befalls kith or kin as you stand watch from
your garden's glen.*

WORRY DOLLS

In these days of constant stress, and for whatever fills your mind with dread or worry, an herbal spell can be just the potion to soothe troubles and heal spirits. Make an herbal poppet specifically to carry your worries away and give your mind a much-needed rest. To get you started, fill or decorate your worry doll with:

- Angelica, garlic, mistletoe, or Himalayan salt to increase feelings of safety, security, and protection

- Basil for money woes

- Cardamom to stir feelings of love, lust, and fidelity, if jealousy rules your heart

- Chamomile for restful sleep

- Dill or fennel to quiet bad dreams in children

- Dried acorns to reverse worries about aging

- Geranium to help ease tension in the body

- Ginger to relieve the effects of general stress on the body

- Hops to hop on the dreamland express

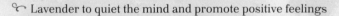

- Lavender to quiet the mind and promote positive feelings
- Lemon balm to clear the cobwebs
- Marigold if legal troubles loom large
- Motherwort to press "pause" on rising panic
- Passionflower to ease chronic worry
- Peppermint to soothe tension headaches
- Rose petals for love woes and healing
- Rosemary to boost the healing love received from others and rejuvenate energy if stress is sapping yours
- Sage to ease grief
- St. John's wort to lift depression
- Star anise for overall feelings of calm and protection from the evil eye, it that's your worry
- Thyme to help you feel grounded
- Verbena to promote peaceful feelings
- Violet to let go of frustration
- Ylang-ylang to reduce overall anxiety and improve libido

Give your worries over to your personal worry doll, to help heal what harms your spirit. Whisper your fears to your worry doll, ask for its help with the outcome you desire, place it beneath your pillow, where they will be absorbed and resolved as you drift gently off to sleep.

JUNE 2023

NOTES	SUNDAY	MONDAY	TUESDAY
	4	5	6
	11	12	13
○	18	19	20
	FATHER'S DAY (US/CAN/UK)	JUNETEENTH (US)	
	25 ◗	26	27

JUNE 2023

WEDNESDAY	THURSDAY	FRIDAY	SATURDAY
	1 FIRST DAY OF PRIDE MONTH	2	3
7	8	9	10
14 FLAG DAY (US)	15	16	17
21 SUMMER SOLSTICE	22	23	24
28	29	30	

STAR ANISE | *Illicium verum*

PLANETARY COMPANIONS MOON, JUPITER	**DAILY CORRESPONDENCE** MONDAY, THURSDAY
ZODIAC SIGNS Sagittarius, Pisces	**ELEMENT** AIR
ENERGY MASCULINE	

With its message of joy and positivity, star anise is a favorite kitchen herb, used in foods as diverse as liqueurs, cookies, Chinese five-spice powder, pho, sausage, chai, and jellies. Originating from Southwest China, and a regular commodity along the spice trade routes, star anise was used medicinally by ancient Chinese herbalists. Today, there is a component of the spice that is used in the flu-fighting medicine Tamiflu. A pod (star) with more than eight points is considered especially lucky. Do not confuse this herb with Japanese star anise, which is toxic.

MAGICAL PROPERTIES
Star anise brings luck, increases psychic intuition, aids in purification rituals, and brings on a state of happiness.

SUGGESTED USE
Raise the energies on your altar by placing star anise in its corners. Carry star anise for luck and protection against the evil eye. Tuck some into a dream sachet for intuitive dreams, or steep one with your tea or chai for a slight licorice flavor as well as an intuition boost, or simmer a few in a pot of water on the stovetop for same. Let the water cool when done and use it for cleaning your altar. Include in incense for purification and intention setting; season food liberally for pure happiness. Add to potpourri not only for its scent and cleansing energies, but also for its delightful shape and calming influence.

O' fragrant herbal star, shine your protective light on me.
When placed upon my altar I do humbly ask of thee,
that intentions set upon this place return to me by three.

MONDAY (MAY) SPRING BANK HOLIDAY (UK) / MEMORIAL DAY (US) **29**

TUESDAY (MAY) **30**

WEDNESDAY (MAY) **31**

THURSDAY FIRST DAY OF PRIDE MONTH **1**

FRIDAY **2**

SATURDAY **3**

SUNDAY **4**

JUNE 2023

MONDAY 5

TUESDAY 6

WEDNESDAY 7

THURSDAY 8

FRIDAY   9

SATURDAY   10

SUNDAY   11

I wish to know now my betrothed,
please yarrow tell me who.
I wear your blossoms on my heart that
they reveal somehow the one who's meant
to marry me, I'll pledge my whole troth to.

JUNE 2023

MONDAY 12

TUESDAY 13

WEDNESDAY FLAG DAY (US) 14

THURSDAY 15

FRIDAY 16

SATURDAY 17

○ **SUNDAY** 18

*With tarragon in hand, a dragon-slayer I become
to conquer fears that keep me from the life I need to
own. O' sword-like leaves of tarragon, cut through
the troubled noise and light the fire within my heart
to burn with courage and joy.*

MONDAY JUNETEENTH HOLIDAY 19

TUESDAY 20

WEDNESDAY SUMMER SOLSTICE 21

THURSDAY 22

FRIDAY 23

SATURDAY 24

SUNDAY 25

An orchid's beauty must be seen—its gift too rare to hide. With orchid placed upon my wrist I gain a sense of pride, to see my beauty recognized, brought forth for all to shine.

WEDDING WISHES

Weddings are the perfect time to express and celebrate the hopes, dreams, and plans for the new couple with plants, flowers, and herbs, to express gratitude to the families and wedding party and celebrate the formation of a new family. Planning arrangements with your secret messages embedded within can be a memorable way to share the love and commitment of the day. A decoding menu would make a lovely keepsake.

Use herbs, plants, and flowers in tabletop decorations, as buffet garnishes, as ingredients in the foods served, and in cocktails. Send seed paper with your wedding invitations. Bundle specific herbs and flowers in the wedding party's bouquets and boutonnieres. Give special posies to family to honor their meaning in your life. Decorate the wedding cake, the venue, or use Nature's hall—a lovely park, beach, glen, or forest—for the ceremony. Include an arrangement of special sentiment for friends and family unable to be with you. Create a wedding potpourri using your favorite herbs to shower the wedding couple with, whether for the message or scent. Potpourri bags would also make lovely wedding favors. Dried herbs and flowers adorning the wedding invitation in a special frame is a meaningful wedding gift.

You may even consider preserving some special herbs and flowers that speak of love and thanks to include in thank-you notes afterward.

In the language of flowers, consider:

- Apple blossom or forget-me-not, for true love
- Basil, for good wishes
- Bellflower, for constancy and gratitude
- Carnation, for admiration and affection
- Dill, for good spirits
- Dwarf sunflower, for adoration
- Fern, for fascination
- Hawthorn, for hope
- Hibiscus, for delicate beauty
- Holly or vervain (verbena), for enchantment
- Honeysuckle or lavender, for generous and devoted affection
- Houseleeks, for vivacity

- Ivy, veronica, cumin, cardamom, or red clover, for fidelity
- Jasmine, for sensuality
- Lemon balm, for sweet memories
- Marjoram, for blushes
- Mint, for warm feelings
- Moss, for maternal love
- Mugwort, for happiness
- Myrtle, for love
- Orange blossom, for marital festivity
- Oregano, for joy
- Oxeye daisy, for patience
- Parsley, for festivity
- Pineapple, for perfection
- Purple lilac, for first emotions of love
- Ranunculus, for radiant charm
- Red rose or red tulip, for a declaration of love
- Rosemary, for fidelity, loyalty, and remembrance
- Rose-scented geranium, for preference
- Sage, for long life and good health
- Thyme, for courage
- Viola, for happy thoughts
- Violet, for faithfulness
- Witch hazel, for a love spell
- Yarrow, for everlasting love
- Zinnia, for thoughts of absent friends

With herbal muse to speak for me the words come fast and free.

To cherish, honor, love, uphold all those so dear to me,

that as I form a union new, the old stays part of me.

JULY 2023

NOTES	SUNDAY	MONDAY	TUESDAY
	2 ●	3	4
			INDEPENDENCE DAY (US)
	◑ 9	10	11
	16 ○	17	18
	23	24 ◖	25
	30	31	

JULY 2023

WEDNESDAY	THURSDAY	FRIDAY	SATURDAY
			1 CANADA DAY (CAN)
5	6	7	8
12	13	14	15
19	20	21	22
26	27	28	29

SWEET PEA BLOSSOM | *Lathyrus odoratus*

PLANETARY COMPANION **VENUS**	DAILY CORRESPONDENCE **FRIDAY**
ZODIAC SIGNS Libra, Taurus	ELEMENT **EARTH**
ENERGY **FEMININE**	

Developed during the Victorian era, this sweetly scented plant is a favorite in English cottage gardens and cutting gardens. Sweet pea blossom says good-bye and signals impending departure in the language of flowers. Though sweet pea bears a strong resemblance to garden peas, do not eat any part of the plant—it is toxic. This plant is grown for its enticing scent.

MAGICAL PROPERTIES
Sweet pea attracts true friends, protects children, and brings good luck.

SUGGESTED USE
Offer a fragrant bouquet, whose stems have been cut in the morning, to an acquaintance you wish to know well, and new friendship will be born. Pin the sweet blossoms to a poppet to offer protection from illness and evil for any children in your life. Pin the flowers to your lapel, or wear in your hair, to encourage luck to stick by your side. Inhale their lovely fragrance as these flowers grow in your garden and be inspired to pay it forward with no expectation of reward.

This lovely plant so freely gives its joyous gift—its scent.
If each of us, I'll start with me, returned the sweet intent,
the world would full of angels be, direct from heaven sent.

MONDAY (JUNE) 26

TUESDAY (JUNE) 27

WEDNESDAY (JUNE) 28

THURSDAY (JUNE) 29

FRIDAY (JUNE) 30

SATURDAY CANADA DAY (CAN) 1

SUNDAY 2

JULY 2023

MONDAY 3

TUESDAY INDEPENDENCE DAY (US) 4

WEDNESDAY 5

THURSDAY 6

FRIDAY 7

SATURDAY 8

◗ **SUNDAY** 9

Oregano—sprinkle my life with joy;
I've a sprig here for luck to employ.
Season each day with happiness, pray,
and fill it with love from above.

JULY 2023

MONDAY 10

TUESDAY 11

WEDNESDAY 12

THURSDAY 13

FRIDAY 14

SATURDAY 15

SUNDAY 16

*As now I lay me down to sleep, I pray
this herbal pillow keeps bad dreams and
nightmares from my head, with peaceful
dreams to lull instead.*

JULY 2023

○ MONDAY   17

TUESDAY   18

WEDNESDAY   19

THURSDAY   20

FRIDAY   **21**

SATURDAY   **22**

SUNDAY   **23**

My sleeping babe, most treasured sight,
this mallow by your crib tonight,
does spirits calm, with soothing balm,
and keeps you safe from any harm.

MONDAY 24

TUESDAY 25

WEDNESDAY 26

THURSDAY 27

FRIDAY 28

SATURDAY 29

SUNDAY 30

*O' bloom whose charms do so delight, I seek
your counsel wise, do tell of love or fond
delight within my lover's eyes. Am I the cause
of such desire, or elsewhere does it lie?*

I AM ME AND I AM ENOUGH

When that nagging voice in your head is wearing you down, it's time to act to still the voice and conjure confidence. Call on the power of the Sun and any number of Sun-correspondence herbs, such as angelica, bay laurel, black tea, chamomile, cinnamon, frankincense, ginseng, marigold, mistletoe, orange blossom, rosemary, St. John's wort, or turmeric.

Each and every herb created by Nature is a perfect living thing—just like you. Each and every herb has its perfect traits and talents—just like you. Each and every herb will in turn boost another just by its existence—just like you. Nature is beautiful and perfect—just like you.

REPELLING EVIL SPIRITS

When moving into a new space, or after an argument, an illness, losing a job, or other negativity-inducing event in your home, it's likely you'll feel the stagnant energy affecting everything you do. Sometimes, you just want it to be fresh and clean to welcome guests, or a new baby or pet, into the environment with ease and joy. Whatever your cause to refresh and rebalance the energies in your home so its inhabitants thrive, several herbs can be helpful.

A few suggestions: chives, cloves, dill, feverfew, ginger, lemon balm, pine, sage, St. John's wort, thyme, and witch hazel are particularly effective allies in clearing negativity and inviting in the positive. In addition, Saturn herbs, and performing any spell or smudge on Saturday, will boost the charge.

Select the herbs you want to work with, take a moment to visualize the space filled with clean bright light, and, when ready, say quietly or aloud:

With these herbs plucked from the Earth

and filled with the power to banish,

I cast these words with most fervent urge

to cleanse, clear, and halt evil spirits.

With wave of their leaves I restore peace and ease

that life does repair, heal, and flourish.

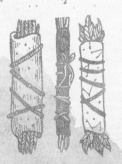

AUGUST 2023

NOTES	SUNDAY	MONDAY	TUESDAY
			● 1
	6	7 ◐	8
	13	14	15
	20	21	22
	27	28 SUMMER BANK HOLIDAY (UK-ENG/NIR/WAL)	29

AUGUST 2023

WEDNESDAY	THURSDAY	FRIDAY	SATURDAY
2	3	4	5
9	10	11	12
○ 16	17	18	19
23	◑ 24	25	26
● 30	31		

VERVAIN (VERBENA) | *Verbena officinalis*

PLANETARY COMPANION **VENUS**	**DAILY CORRESPONDENCE** **FRIDAY**
ZODIAC SIGNS **Cancer, Gemini, Libra, Taurus**	**ELEMENT** **EARTH**
ENERGY **FEMININE**	

Vervain symbolizes protection, happiness, and creativity. It also speaks of enchantment. It was a favorite herb of the Druids, who gathered it at night under the light of summer's Dog Star for use in ritual cleansing and purification, for which it boasts a long history among many cultures. It is said to be connected to the Underworld and may help call to departed souls. It was used as a magic wand by every self-respecting magician, witch, and warlock in times past. Placed in a baby's crib, it instills a lifelong love of learning and a sunny disposition.

MAGICAL PROPERTIES
Vervain offers protection and calming energies, fosters good communication, alleviates stress, and brings about happiness and prosperity.

SUGGESTED USE
Add an infusion to a ritual bath for cleansing and to induce telling dreams. Hang branches above doorways to guard against evil entering. Try a tea to boost creativity. Include in flower arrangements to engender happiness. Add to sachets for prosperity spells.

My altar swept with vervain branch; with water I do cleanse.
Prepared I am to call on truth to tell its unheard tale—
to speak of things now yet unknown but must, in light, prevail.

MONDAY (JULY) 31

TUESDAY 1

WEDNESDAY 2

THURSDAY 3

FRIDAY 4

SATURDAY 5

SUNDAY 6

AUGUST 2023

MONDAY 7

TUESDAY 8

WEDNESDAY 9

THURSDAY 10

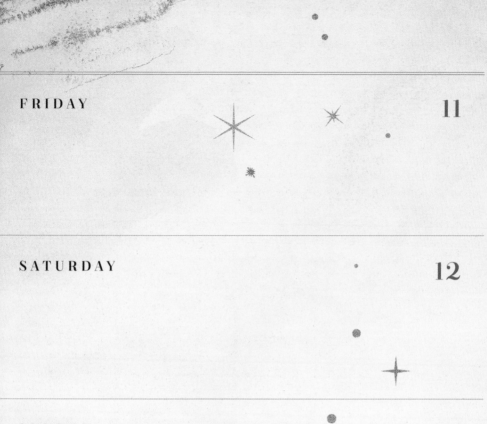

FRIDAY   11

SATURDAY   12

SUNDAY   13

*There is no time to dilly-dally; it's love
I seek today. With seed, and leaf, and
root of dill, I hungrily do pray that
romance and its courting dance do
hurry here my way.*

MONDAY 14

TUESDAY 15

○ WEDNESDAY 16

THURSDAY 17

FRIDAY 18

SATURDAY 19

SUNDAY 20

When cats do cry and birds do fly and
blackened clouds do fill the sky, I light this herb
to clear the air that only those who enter here
bring peace and joy and soothing ways, and
evil fast and far does fly.

AUGUST 2023

MONDAY 21

TUESDAY 22

WEDNESDAY 23

THURSDAY 24

FRIDAY 25

SATURDAY 26

SUNDAY 27

Of mint or lime and chocolate, too, sweet
geranium's scents my stress undo. For when
I pass this charming plant, its calming scents
do cool the rant that on my way, thus soothed
I'll be, for life is short: live happily!

PROTECTIVE WREATH

Made from natural materials, such as herbs, twigs, flowers, and more, wreaths are more than decorative and have served many purposes throughout time. The wreath, an unending circle, symbolizes eternity and the cycle of the seasons. Hanging a wreath on your door can also be a symbol of protection for the home. Customize your wreath based on your intentions and take advantage of seasonal materials, such as herbs in your garden, to refresh and boost the energies you'd like to raise.

Using these protective herbs, dress up and protect your home with the energies of the seasons:

- Angelica
- Basil
- Bay laurel
- Chives
- Dill
- Fern
- Foxglove
- Holly
- Mugwort
- Oak leaves and acorns
- Rosemary
- Rowan
- Sage
- Star anise
- Witch hazel

I cast this circle on my door, with herbs so rich and deep in lore,

that from all ills protected be,

my home will ne'er be harmed nor poor.

EXTINGUISHING BAD HABITS

Sometimes, our bad habits can keep us from reaching our goals, whether losing weight, finishing that home project, healing a family rift, or gaining that promotion at work, and we frequently undermine our true intentions. When the time is right to commit to achieving your goals, you may have to commit to extinguishing the behavior getting in your way.

Bay laurel and chives are solid allies in helping break bad habits. Tie a bundle of bay leaves with a few chives and place it on your altar. Call on the energy of Saturn, on a Saturday, and any of Saturn's herbs, such as comfrey, ivy—especially good at capturing negative energy in its tangled growth— morning glory, mullein, thyme, or viola. Add a rose quartz, or burn a pink candle, for self-love.

Acknowledge the habit you'll work hard to break, then take a few moments to visualize reaching your goals, feeling the pride of accomplishment. When ready, say quietly or aloud:

Good herbs do join this fearsome fight

to keep my worthy goals in sight

and wick away the habits rued that fail to help me win the right

to cheer and brag when I am through, each hope and dream

achieving true.

SEPTEMBER 2023

NOTES	SUNDAY	MONDAY	TUESDAY
	3	**4**	**5**
	FATHER'S DAY (AUS/NZ)	LABOR DAY (US) LABOUR DAY (CAN)	
	10	**11**	**12**
	GRANDPARENTS' DAY (US)	PATRIOT DAY (US)	
	17	**18**	**19**
	24	**25**	**26**
	YOM KIPPUR (BEGINS AT SUNDOWN)		

SEPTEMBER 2023

WEDNESDAY	THURSDAY	FRIDAY	SATURDAY
		1	2
☽ 6	7	8	9
13 ○	14	15 ROSH HASHANAH (BEGINS AT SUNDOWN) FIRST DAY OF NATIONAL HISPANIC HERITAGE MONTH	16
20	21 ☽	22	23 FALL EQUINOX
27	28 ●	29 SUKKOT (BEGINS AT SUNDOWN)	30

WITCH HAZEL | *Hamamelis virginiana*

PLANETARY COMPANION **SUN**	DAILY CORRESPONDENCE **SUNDAY**
ZODIAC SIGNS **Aquarius, Leo**	ELEMENT **FIRE**
ENERGY **MASCULINE**	

One of the first plants to bloom near winter's end, witch hazel is an uplifting sight. Famously known to offer the best wood for divining rods—useful for finding water or gold—witch hazel can help cast a spell. This herb is a popular ingredient in personal care products, including the original formula for Pond's cold cream.

MAGICAL PROPERTIES
Protective against the evil eye and harmful spirits, witch hazel is also a potent energizer in love spells and a healer of broken hearts if love goes wrong. It can restore emotional balance when strong emotions flare.

SUGGESTED USE
Instead of smudging, wave a branch or two of witch hazel throughout your home, paying special attention to doorways, closets, corners, and windows, to expel negative energies and evil forces. Dress any candle used for love spells with witch hazel oil. Fill a healing poppet with leaves and flowers or add to any healing spell or spell jar. Plant witch hazel on your property for its protective aura, or keep its flowering branches on your altar and add blooms to any protective charms. Its affinity for finding water, as well as treasure, also makes witch hazel a good companion for weather spells.

The rain is needed desperately to give the Earth a break.
Witch hazel, spread your branches wide and call upon the sky:
Assemble clouds and lightning proud to shed their healing tears
so, when it's done, the Earth's great thirst will fully have been slaked.

AUGUST/SEPTEMBER 2023

MONDAY (AUGUST) SUMMER BANK HOLIDAY (UK-ENG/NIR/WAL) **28**

TUESDAY (AUGUST) **29**

WEDNESDAY (AUGUST) **30**

THURSDAY (AUGUST) **31**

FRIDAY **1**

SATURDAY **2**

SUNDAY FATHER'S DAY (AUS/NZ) **3**

SEPTEMBER 2023

MONDAY LABOR DAY (US) / LABOUR DAY (CAN)

4

TUESDAY

5

WEDNESDAY

6

THURSDAY

7

FRIDAY 8

SATURDAY 9

SUNDAY GRANDPARENTS' DAY (US) 10

Each day goes faster than the other;
I'd like to live to be one hundred. With
tansy planted by my door, may health hold
fast and my years be more.

SEPTEMBER 2023

MONDAY PATRIOT DAY (US) 11

TUESDAY 12

WEDNESDAY 13

○ THURSDAY 14

FRIDAY ROSH HASHANAH (BEGINS AT SUNDOWN) /
FIRST DAY OF NATIONAL HISPANIC
HERITAGE MONTH

15

SATURDAY

16

SUNDAY

17

*Of hale and hardy health am I and like
so wish to stay—like an apple a day,
turmeric's spicy ways heal what ails
like the Sun's shining rays.*

SEPTEMBER 2023 ✦

MONDAY 18

TUESDAY 19

WEDNESDAY 20

THURSDAY 21

FRIDAY

22

SATURDAY FALL EQUINOX

23

SUNDAY YOM KIPPUR (BEGINS AT SUNDOWN)

24

When lacking courage to face the day,
I call on thyme to ease my way. For courage
in battles, big and small, foretells good
outcomes—one and all.

A TOAST TO SUCCESS

For this spell, it's handy to have some fresh herb-studded ice cubes to help boost the good vibes—but garnishing with any fresh herbs added to your favorite cheer-boosting beverage will do in a pinch. Add these charming cubes to any beverage to infuse them with herbal magic and good cheer. For fun, and some additional flavor, pair your herbs and flowers with pieces of fruit, such as citrus, berries, pineapple, or cranberries.

Good herbs for prosperity, hidden worth, and luck include basil, bergamot, comfrey, coriander, nutmeg, and vervain. The language of flowers speaks of fame and good reputation through apple blossom, bachelor's button for love and blessings, and borage for courage.

GATHER:
Herb sprigs, blossoms, and leaves to honor your intentions
Edible flowers to speak the language of good fortune
2 or more ice-cube trays
Chopstick (optional)

1. Make sure the herbs and flowers you're using are free from dirt and debris. Give them a quick rinse, if needed, and dry well. Arrange whole leaves, herbal blossoms, sprig pieces, or edible flower heads and petals decoratively in the tray compartments.

2. Gently fill the trays about one-third to one-half full of water. Use the chopstick to reposition the herbs and flowers, as desired, if the water disturbed your arrangement. Carefully transfer the trays to the freezer and freeze for about 1 hour.

3. Fill the trays the remaining way with water and freeze until solid.

With beverage in hand and intentions in heart, imagine the good fortune you seek. When ready, say quietly or aloud:

Let's toast to fortunes great and small, may either come my way.

Sweet herbal charms, whose message sends

three cheers for luck this day,

refresh my glass, refill my hopes, success is here to stay.

FACING FEARS

Sometimes fear of failure, or operating outside our comfort zone, can create uncomfortable feelings that freeze us in our tracks. When you suspect your procrastination, or fear of taking action, comes from a deeper place, acknowledge it and face it. Take one deep breath and two steps forward and you will soon forget what was holding your back!

Gather any or all these herbs for courage: basil, black pepper, borage, dandelion, garlic, holly, lavender, lemon thyme, motherwort, mullein, oregano, St. John's wort, tarragon, or violet. Create a worry doll, transfer the worry to your worry companion, and free your mind to resolve your fears.

Holding your worry doll close to your heart, say quietly:

I whisper soft my fears to you, for said aloud they may prove true.

Please, worry friend, do take these fears

and carry them away from here.

And herbs of courage do fill my heart

with strength to do and will to start

a fearless pace to reach my goals and gratitude to fill my soul.

OCTOBER 2023

NOTES	SUNDAY	MONDAY	TUESDAY
	1	2 LABOUR DAY (AUS-ACT/NSW/SA)	3
	8	9 INDIGENOUS PEOPLES' DAY (US) COLUMBUS DAY (US) THANKSGIVING DAY (CAN)	10
	15	16	17
	22	23 LABOUR DAY (NZ)	24
	29	30	31 HALLOWEEN

OCTOBER 2023

WEDNESDAY	THURSDAY	FRIDAY	SATURDAY
4	5 ◗	6	7
			SIMCHAT TORAH (BEGINS AT SUNDOWN)
11	12	13	○ 14
18	19	20 ◖	21
25	26	27 ●	28

PATCHOULI | *Pogostemon cablin*

PLANETARY COMPANION **MARS**	DAILY CORRESPONDENCE **TUESDAY**
ZODIAC SIGNS **Libra, Taurus, Virgo**	ELEMENT **EARTH**
ENERGY **FEMININE**	

Patchouli's earthy smell is often an acquired taste but may be worth it for those looking for luck in the areas of love and money. Its exotic scent, often included in perfumes and potpourris and used as incense, has an otherworldly quality that can enchant your spellwork. Its language is passion.

MAGICAL PROPERTIES
Patchouli is well known for its ability to attract money. Though not entirely related, it's also used as an aphrodisiac and to aid fertility.

SUGGESTED USE
Utilize in love and money spells for best results. Consider a spritz of patchouli cologne before your next casino outing. Add to a ritual bath, or use a perfumed soap, to open your intuitive pathways.

No need to "roll the dice" when patchouli's in the house.
Three dabs upon the wrist and Lady Luck it does arouse.

SEPTEMBER / OCTOBER 2023

MONDAY (SEPTEMBER)   25

TUESDAY (SEPTEMBER)   26

WEDNESDAY (SEPTEMBER)   27

THURSDAY (SEPTEMBER)   28

● FRIDAY (SEPTEMBER) SUKKOT (BEGINS AT SUNDOWN)   29

SATURDAY (SEPTEMBER)   30

SUNDAY   1

OCTOBER 2023

MONDAY LABOUR DAY (AUS-ACT/NSW/SA) 2

TUESDAY 3

WEDNESDAY 4

THURSDAY 5

FRIDAY   6

SATURDAY SIMCHAT TORAH (BEGINS AT SUNDOWN)   7

SUNDAY   8

With violet posy tucked close by, a wish
for all my friends that steadfast love
endures the times unable we're to tend
the faithful friendships that we yearn to
last until the end.

OCTOBER 2023

MONDAY   INDIGENOUS PEOPLES' DAY (US) /
         COLUMBUS DAY (US) / THANKSGIVING DAY (CAN)   9

TUESDAY   10

WEDNESDAY   11

THURSDAY   12

FRIDAY

13

○ **SATURDAY**

14

SUNDAY

15

For craps or slots, and poker, too, rub lucky
nutmeg in my shoe. When carried, worn, and
sprinkled on, this spicy herb turns on the charm
if dice are cold and slots don't hit, it's nutmeg's
chance to work the pit to turn your luck from cold
to hot and guarantee you'll cry, "Jackpot!"

OCTOBER 2023

MONDAY 16

TUESDAY 17

WEDNESDAY 18

THURSDAY 19

FRIDAY 20

SATURDAY 21

SUNDAY 22

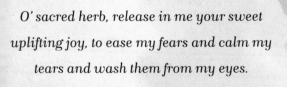

O' sacred herb, release in me your sweet uplifting joy, to ease my fears and calm my tears and wash them from my eyes.

OCTOBER 2023

MONDAY LABOUR DAY (NZ)   **23**

TUESDAY   **24**

WEDNESDAY   **25**

THURSDAY   **26**

FRIDAY   27

● SATURDAY   28

SUNDAY   29

With racing thoughts that need a rest,
a sprinkle of cardamom in my chai
does have its sweet effect on me.
With one inhale of scented steam that clears
the mind, restores the dream, I'm back
to who I was meant to be.

ORANGE BLOSSOM-HIBISCUS SALT SOAK

Sometimes a little sunshine can chase away the blues faster than anything else. Emerge from this bath soothed and uplifted with a dose of these sunny salts, which can also reduce itching, relieve minor arthritis pain, soothe swollen feet, and help ease pulled muscles, which may be lurking in the background. Incorporate orange crystals or candles to raise the happiness factor, or pink crystals or candles to affirm your goddess charms and celebrate your natural beauty.

GATHER:

2 cups (500 g) Epsom salt
Neroli essential oil
2 teaspoons carrier oil (jojoba, sweet almond)
¼ cup (10 g) dried hibiscus blossoms
Fresh orange blossoms, for floating in the tub (optional)

1. Pour 1 cup (250 g) of Epsom salt into a 1-pint (480-ml) Mason jar.

2. Add 20 drops of neroli essential oil, or more as you like, and the carrier oil. Seal the lid and shake to blend the scent with the salt.

3. Add the hibiscus blossoms and remaining 1 cup (250 g) of Epsom salt. Re-cover the jar and shake to combine everything. Label and date your salt soak and keep stored in a cool, dark place.

4. Shake before adding 1 to 2 cups (250 to 500 g) to a warm bath. If lucky enough to have them, float the orange blossoms on the sweetly scented water, ease into the tub, and feel the joy surround you.

To lift the gloomy clouds that haunt, I seek the help

of scented salt, when coupled with the water's ease,

the darkness shifts on sunny breeze.

SOOTHING FACIAL STEAM

Feeling your best can get a huge boost when you're looking your best. As part of a regular cleansing regimen for your face, an herbal steam is an easy at-home spa treatment that can help stimulate circulation and eliminate toxins—and put your best face forward. The scent, moisture, and herbal properties cleanse and soothe. This 15-minute treatment can also be combined with a spell of mindful meditation to double the magical outcomes.

1. Cleanse your face as normal.

2. Place a large heatproof bowl on a heatproof surface at a height that is comfortable for you to sit near and bend your head over (12 to 18 inches, or 30 to 45 cm, above the bowl).

3. Fill the bowl with 2 or 3 handfuls of fresh herbs or 2 to 4 tablespoons (weight varies) of dried herbs. Add a drop of essential oil, if you like.

4. Pour in about 4 cups (960 ml) of boiling water. Take a moment to acknowledge the gifts of the Earth.

5. Hold your face, eyes closed, over the steaming herbal mixture, and place a towel over your head and the bowl to capture the aromatic, cleansing steam. Relax into the scent and senses for about 15 minutes, or until the steam dissipates. Use the time to focus on your breath to instill a sense of peace and calm, or to set intentions based on the herbal steam you're inhaling.

6. Finish with a cool water rinse and pat dry. As you prepare the steam with the herbs and water, call on their energies to heal:

To clear the mind and cleanse the face,

I call on water's soothing grace.

With herbal powers thus enjoined to wick away the dirt and grime,

I'm left with beauty fresh and free to face the day with dignity.

NOVEMBER 2023

NOTES	SUNDAY	MONDAY	TUESDAY
	◗ 5	6	7
	DAYLIGHT SAVING TIME ENDS (US/CAN)		ELECTION DAY (US)
	12	○ 13	14
	19	◖ 20	21
	26	● 27	28

NOVEMBER 2023

WEDNESDAY	THURSDAY	FRIDAY	SATURDAY
1 ALL SAINTS' DAY	2	3	4
8	9	10	11 VETERANS DAY (US)
15	16	17	18
22	23 THANKSGIVING DAY (US)	24 NATIVE AMERICAN HERITAGE DAY (US)	25
29	30		

NASTURTIUM | *Tropaeolum majus*

PLANETARY COMPANION	DAILY CORRESPONDENCE
MARS	**TUESDAY**
ZODIAC SIGN	ELEMENTS
Libra	**AIR, FIRE**
ENERGY	
FEMININE	

In the language of flowers, nasturtium means patriotism. This small, peppery-tasting plant can add zip to the otherwise dull salad, and color to bring on cheer.

MAGICAL PROPERTIES
Nasturtium can help rid the mind of fear and cleanse the air of negativity. It fosters a sense of creativity and individuality. It breeds loyalty, aids in conquest, and, through its message of patriotism, encourages a sense of community and harmony in working together.

SUGGESTED USE
Add blossoms to a bath for a purifying, cleansing effect. Incorporate into a potpourri to raise the magical vibrations in your home and invite in a little fun. Add petals to a salad to liven the discussion and foster family harmony. Tuck into a wreath or flower arrangement to add an element of encouragement.

These blossoms bright, I call on you to boldly spark a change,
from fear and fright to newfound heights where
my voice does clearly ring.

OCTOBER/NOVEMBER 2023

MONDAY (OCTOBER) 30

TUESDAY (OCTOBER) HALLOWEEN 31

WEDNESDAY ALL SAINTS' DAY 1

THURSDAY 2

FRIDAY 3

SATURDAY 4

SUNDAY DAYLIGHT SAVING TIME ENDS (US/CAN) 5

NOVEMBER 2023

MONDAY   6

TUESDAY   ELECTION DAY (US)   7

WEDNESDAY   8

THURSDAY   9

FRIDAY

10

SATURDAY VETERANS DAY (US)

11

SUNDAY

12

Of calming hue and soothing scent, please,
lavender, sing your song—A lullaby—a
balm of notes—with which to sing along,
To carry me to 'yon new day, restored,
renewed, and strong.

NOVEMBER 2023

○ MONDAY   13

TUESDAY   14

WEDNESDAY   15

THURSDAY   16

FRIDAY 17

SATURDAY 18

SUNDAY 19

With lady's mantle dew so rare, upon my
face that I do dare believe its beauty will
outshine, all those who seek my lover's
time. I call upon this dew sublime to call
my lover's heart to mine.

November 2023

MONDAY — **20**

TUESDAY — **21**

WEDNESDAY — **22**

THURSDAY THANKSGIVING DAY (US) — **23**

FRIDAY NATIVE AMERICAN HERITAGE DAY (US)   24

SATURDAY   25

SUNDAY   26

As ginseng root grows long and deep,
its age enhances charm. I call on ginseng's
mystic lore to keep me safe from harm
that long this life of mine may be,
its memories to warm.

FORGIVENESS

Forgiveness, whether of ourselves or others who have hurt us, is the magical balm that can bring about real healing. Our emotional well-being is just as important as our physical well-being, and, in fact, the two influence each other. Several herbs can help ease the work of conjuring true forgiveness in one's heart—they just need to be invited in. Call on basil, ginger, hawthorn, marigold, moonwort, orange blossom, rose, and tarragon to start, alone or in any combination that pleases the senses and emotions. For this special work, be sure to thank the herbs for their healing help and repeat as often as needed.

This herbal blend, my healing friend—a poultice to my soul.

When placed upon the fire that's my smoldering heart of coal,

they smudge the space, invite with grace,

forgiveness to blossom whole.

CELEBRATING DIFFERENCES

The thrilling diversity of the herbal kingdom is something we celebrate and yearn to learn more about, and so it should be with the uplifting diversity of the human kingdom. When differences threaten to divide instead of delight, learning more about them is the first step to understanding differences aren't always as different as they first appear.

Gather cinquefoil, mugwort, sage, and willow for wisdom; morning glory and rosemary for acceptance; sweet pea for friendship; and nasturtium for working in harmony. Invite the wisdom of your favorite goddess in for a chat. When ready to seek common ground, say quietly or aloud:

These herbs in friendship offered are, with purest of intent

to let the conversation flow, to understand what's meant

by words and deeds, to sow the seeds of wisdom

and accept what's different.

DECEMBER 2023

NOTES	SUNDAY	MONDAY	TUESDAY
	3	4 ◑	5
	INTERNATIONAL DAY OF PERSONS WITH DISABILITIES		
	10	11 ○	12
	HUMAN RIGHTS DAY		
	17	18 ◐	19
	24	25 ●	26
	CHRISTMAS EVE		
	31		BOXING DAY (UK/CAN/AUS/NZ)
	NEW YEAR'S EVE	CHRISTMAS DAY	KWANZAA

DECEMBER 2023

WEDNESDAY	THURSDAY	FRIDAY	SATURDAY
		1 WORLD AIDS DAY	2
6	7 HANUKKAH (BEGINS AT SUNDOWN)	8	9
13	14	15	16
20	21 WINTER SOLSTICE	22	23
27	28	29	30

MORNING GLORY | *Ipomoea mauritiana* (vine)

PLANETARY COMPANION
SATURN

DAILY CORRESPONDENCE
SATURDAY

ZODIAC SIGNS
Aquarius, Pisces

ELEMENTS
EARTH, FIRE

ENERGY
MASCULINE

With a slightly sweet scent, but vibrant color, morning glory's vining, clinging habit is especially helpful for joining lovers. In the language of flowers, morning glory speaks of affection. It is related to the moonflower.

MAGICAL PROPERTIES
This trumpet-shaped beauty's magic lies in protection, revealing truth, and acceptance. It brings peace and happiness to all who see it.

SUGGESTED USE
Gather a posy for one you love, or use the morning glory flower in a love spell to communicate with your intended. Gather morning glory seeds in a sachet (reminder: they're poisonous) and place under your pillow to induce clarity-seeking dreams. Their sweet energy will help you see what you need to know and accept the path forward.

As morning glory heralds in another splendid day,
with trumpet call, a sign to all—do hurry, don't delay—
grant me the grace to find my place along life's garden path.

NOVEMBER/DECEMBER 2023

MONDAY (NOVEMBER) — 27

TUESDAY (NOVEMBER) — 28

WEDNESDAY (NOVEMBER) — 29

THURSDAY (NOVEMBER) — 30

FRIDAY WORLD AIDS DAY — 1

SATURDAY — 2

SUNDAY INTERNATIONAL DAY OF PERSONS WITH DISABILITIES — 3

DECEMBER 2023

MONDAY 4

TUESDAY 5

WEDNESDAY 6

THURSDAY HANUKKAH (BEGINS AT SUNDOWN) 7

FRIDAY   8

SATURDAY   9

SUNDAY HUMAN RIGHTS DAY   10

*With ginger tea, a spell, and me combining
into sacred three to call upon the spirit
realm that magic powers do not roam but
triple in intensity to manifest my destiny.*

DECEMBER 2023

MONDAY 11

○ **TUESDAY** 12

WEDNESDAY 13

THURSDAY 14

FRIDAY   **15**

SATURDAY   **16**

SUNDAY   **17**

Feverfew, I rely on you to keep the
germs at bay. As weather turns and
colds and germs do hunker down to
stay. Repel their force—with smiles,
of course—so be it, as I say.

DECEMBER 2023

MONDAY 18

TUESDAY 19

WEDNESDAY 20

THURSDAY WINTER SOLSTICE 21

FRIDAY   22

SATURDAY   23

SUNDAY CHRISTMAS EVE   24

For fertile luck I turn to thee, dear mistletoe that
blooms so free in circumstance less than those
designed to nurture plants like thee.
I strive for life to grow in me as evergreen and
joyously, to nurture life within my womb as
mighty oak supports your bloom.

DECEMBER 2023

MONDAY CHRISTMAS DAY

25

TUESDAY BOXING DAY (UK/CAN/AUS/NZ) / KWANZAA

26

WEDNESDAY

27

THURSDAY

28

FRIDAY   29

SATURDAY   30

SUNDAY NEW YEAR'S EVE   31

I've brewed intent into this tea—a double wish to
bring, for fortune's gone and left me dry, with life
more challenging. With every sip, I thank you for
your truly magic ways, whose luck I reap that
feels a heap like I grabbed the golden ring.

NOTES

NOTES

NOTES

NOTES

NOTES

NOTES

Brimming with creative inspiration, how-to projects, and useful information to enrich your everyday life, quarto.com is a favorite destination for those pursuing their interests and passions.

10 9 8 7 6 5 4 3 2 1

ISBN: 978-1-63106-895-9

Publisher: Rage Kindelsperger
Creative Director: Laura Drew
Managing Editor: Cara Donaldson
Project Editor: Sara Bonacum
Cover and Interior Design: Laura Klynstra
Layout Design: Marisa Kwek

Printed in China

This planner provides general information on various widely known and widely accepted self-care practices. However, it should not be relied upon as recommending or promoting any specific diagnosis or method of treatment for a particular condition, and it is not intended as a substitute for medical advice or for direct diagnosis and treatment of a medical condition by a qualified physician. Readers who have questions about a particular condition, possible treatments for that condition, or possible reactions from the condition or its treatment should consult a physician or other qualified healthcare professional.

All moon phases shown are for the Eastern Time Zone.